CRUSH

Jaimy Blazynski

DEDICATION

I dedicate this book to Erik because I now know that true and undying love really exists. And to Matthew and Trevor, two of the greatest boys on the planet.

CONTENTS

ACKNOWLEDGMENTS

I need to thank my editors Amanda Guay and Tracy Taback for their diligence and support in creating Crush. Thanks also to Shalom Khodabakhshian from ShalomK Photography.

Special thanks to Stefanie Marco, KiNDSPiN DESiGN for her remarkable creativity in delivering the unique cover for Crush.

FORWARD .

In 2005 I started my own dating company called got5minutes.com. The entire purpose of my company is to help those who want to find true love find just that. For many it is a numbers game and they just need to attend a speed dating event. And for those folks I have plenty! For others it may be personal issues. So many singles come to me with fears, negative beliefs, or quite simply just annoying attributes that need to be recognized. For those I offer workshops, discussion groups and individual coaching. And now I have wrapped all of that dating advice into one book, "Crush".

I had no clue in high school or college how to maintain a guy's attention. I did manage to find one willing to marry me and I grabbed on. The relationship ended just after our son Matthew celebrated his first birthday. I blamed my ex-husband for a while and roamed this world angry and scorned. Until that one day I looked at myself in the mirror and thought "YUCK"! My son deserves better. That day I changed my life forever. I recognized all my short comings and took my share of personal responsibility for the marriage ending. I reinvented myself physically and emotionally and for the first time began to like myself and began to believe that I was just as worthy of true love as all of those happy couples that previously made me cringe.

I joined match.com with a positive outlook and put my heart and soul into that search. I knew my deal breakers and wasn't settling for anything less. It was date number 13 that impressed me the most. Sure he was almost five years younger than me and did not have any children of his own. But he was adorable and I knew I was about to have the best summer of my life. This all happened in the summer of

2001. In 2004 we were off to Las Vegas and I walked down the aisle at the Heavenly Bliss Chapel knowing I had finally found my soul mate. Then came Trevor Huck in 2007 and our family was complete!

I still sometimes have to pinch myself to be sure this is all true. I am so proud of my life today. I look back at that angry divorcee who never thought life could be so wonderful and treasure every last second of my life. I hope you will enjoy reliving each and every crush that I am about to share with you. Except for a few names and very minor details these stories are exactly the way I remember them. I enjoyed reliving some more than others but don't have a single regret. Each mistake I made was a lesson learned that brought me to a place of bliss, joy, and love.

"Crush"- According to dictionary.com, this word means "to press or squeeze with a force that destroys or deforms." But how did this term evolve to describe an emotion we have when we fall hard for someone? I imagine this is referring to what happens to one's heart when the crush isn't exactly mutual. Which was the story of my life and the premise of this book.

1 - MATT

Think back to your very first crush for a moment. Am I the only one on the planet that can go all the way back to preschool?

I swear to you, I was only four years old when I had my very first crush. I was forced to go to preschool despite my many attempts to stay home with my mom. His name was Matthew. He was a cute little boy with stringy brownish-red hair that hung right over his beady little blue eyes. He was a little guy but then again we were all little back then. I was cute too, in my preschool days. One would describe me as a skinny, petite girl with a crooked smile, bright blue eyes and two blonde ponytails in my hair. I loved to decorate my hair with ribbons or barrettes and tried to wear the same outfit every day. Whenever my pretty purple dress with my pocket pants and buckle shoes were not clean, I knew I was going to have a bad day.

One memory of this first crush stands out so vividly in my mind. Matthew and I, along with a couple of other preschoolers, were driven to school by a driver named Mr. Lupo. I was not a fan of this arrangement but after losing the battle of having to go to preschool, I knew I didn't stand a chance at winning this debate. One strange day our driver dropped us off at the front entrance of the school, watched us enter the building and drove away. Seems unheard of in this day and age but that was the acceptable routine. Matthew, two other children whose names I don't remember, and I entered the school to find no one was there. The lights were off, the room was dead silent and there was not another living person in sight. I rushed to the door to try to catch Mr. Lupo, our driver. But all I was able to see was the back of the car turning left out of the parking lot. Apparently it was a teacher training day, the school closed and the communication didn't reach the parents or even the drivers that day. We were four-year-old kids left in an empty classroom and quite scared. I stood there frozen and speechless. Matthew walked up to me and held my hand as we all stared in shock at our empty classroom. I forgot about my fear and I was feeling nothing but thrilled that this little boy was holding my hand.

There I was, pondering what this actually meant. I wondered how long we would hold hands. I knew that I was not letting go until he did. No matter how sweaty his little preschooler palm felt, I was happy to hold on. It was just a few minutes before another friend arrived with his mother who actually walked him in to the building. She gathered up our little group of abandoned preschoolers and loaded us into the back of her wood paneled station wagon. Miraculously she figured out our addresses and delivered us home safely.

We all have defining moments in our lives and this may have been my first one. I am not sure if it was that we were all left at an empty preschool or that I had the attention of the first boy that I ever had a crush on.

Matt seemed interested in me for a moment and then never thought about me again. He never joined me at the sand table, never held my hand, didn't notice when I put on the princess costume and never texted me after the date. Oh right - I was supposed to be talking about pre-school. I guess we have moved on to texting and real dates.

Why would a guy hold your hand and even kiss you goodnight if he's not exactly interested in you?

It is very common for the guy to act as if he is interested in seeing you again even if he knows otherwise. He will even go so far as to hold your hand, kiss you good night and tell you what a wonderful time he had.

You walk in the door after the first date (hopefully alone) and feel like this guy is "the one." You obsess over the spark you had, every time you both laughed, and of course that great kiss goodnight. You have been fooled before, but this time there was no indication whatsoever that this would fail. You call your best friend, your mom and your sister to tell them what a great guy he is. You fall asleep with a smile on your face and wake up the next morning eagerly grabbing for your cell phone. Please, oh please, let there be a text or an email... and nothing. OK, so you begin to rationalize that it has only been 10 hours. Give it a few days. Perhaps he is still one of those fools that believe in the three-day rule (which is no longer valid, by the way). With today's technology, a quick text or email within 24 hours is more common and greatly appreciated by the person questioning where this relationship is headed.

But now three days have passed, and you are starting to get panicky. You have compulsively checked your Blackberry a million times and you're ready to throw it out the window. You debate texting him but know that he is capable of contacting you if he is truly interested. So you are left feeling anxious, disappointed and entirely sick of trying to get a read on these guys. You have been fooled again and convince yourself that you are done dating forever. You hide your match.com profile and don't go out for weeks. You feel like you just can't bear to experience this rejection ever again. I know the feeling quite well and went though it many times since my crush as a four-year-old.

Now, I will tell you exactly what went wrong. In most cases absolutely nothing went wrong. I wasn't on the date so if you had some crazy dramatic episode or talked incessantly, then perhaps you have your issues. But in most cases if you think the guy had a great time and showed an interest, then I am going to bet that he liked you enough to have an enjoyable evening, but for whatever reason you just weren't "the one" for him.

I know that hurts, because we as women want to believe that we are desirable to everyone. We have a ridiculous fear that if one man doesn't find us hot then no man will. This is not true, and we will learn more about chemistry later in this book. As far as the kiss goodnight goes, some guys are able to show an interest and enjoy a kiss even when they know you are not "the one."

As women, many of us wouldn't dare consider engaging in a kiss goodnight with a guy we weren't interested in.

Maybe a handshake but even that can feel painful. In fact we couldn't even fake enough interest to make the date a comfortable experience. Sometimes we spend most of the date making excuses why he shouldn't pursue you. You have been on match.com for two months, and all of a sudden you are trying to convince your first date that you are not ready to date after all.

Guys handle a lack of interest quite differently. Some are afraid of the drama that would come from the honesty, while others genuinely enjoy your company and just don't want to "close the deal" with you. It would be nice if he could just say, "Thanks for a fun night, but you're just not the right one for me." But honestly, there are some ladies that would be freaked out by this directness.

I know you want to climb into this book and convince me you would thank them for their honesty and go home. But I don't think you all would really do this. Although I do agree that quite a few would be relieved to know the truth and avoid any waiting games. But it is the drama queens that put the fear in these guys and this is why they are so hard to read. Sorry ladies, I am brutally honest and you don't always have to agree with me, but this is my book, so hear me out.

If this is how guys behave then how will I know when the guy is really into me?

As a rule you should never get too excited after just one date. Guys are so hard to read sometimes, and trust me when I tell you that when the guy is interested in you, it will become blatantly obvious. You won't have to wonder when he will call, you won't be surveying all of your friends as to whether or not you should send him a text and you won't be playing games. In fact, I am going to tell you exactly what it should look like. You go on a date with a guy and have a nice time. He kisses you goodnight and you actually like it. You don't cringe but you show some self-control and go home by yourself. He texts you and asks if you got home safely. He calls you within a day or two and you plan a second a date. You both arrive on time and excited to spend time together again.

This continues as you get to know each other better and better. You think about him often, but not in an anxious way. When you talk about him you can't stop smiling. He treats you with the utmost respect. You are not afraid to call him because you have something to share. You aren't wondering if you are being too pushy, or whose turn it is to call. You actually feel happy and excited when he pops in your mind. He begins to call daily to hear your voice, say hello and see how your day was. He begins spending the night and your relationship moves from casually dating to the falling-in-love stage.

You don't get tired or bored of each other after a month. You don't start questioning whether or not he is the right guy for you or if you are settling. You also don't spend endless hours waiting for the phone to ring, making excuses for why he might not be calling or wondering what you may have done wrong. Trust me when I tell you that if a guy is interested in you, he didn't lose your number, he isn't thinking you are not interested in him and he isn't too busy with work. If he is interested he gets in touch with you and the relationship progresses. You may think this is unrealistic but it is happening all of the time!

So in a nutshell, what exactly should I do?

Don't accept anything less than what we described above. If you are just so eager to have some semblance of a relationship that you pursue one that is unclear and complicated, then you will only hinder your chances of meeting the guy that won't play games. Stop convincing yourself that you need to settle and get back out there - and don't sacrifice anything this time! Being single and available is so much better (and so much more fun) than being trapped in a miserable or unsatisfying relationship.

2 - DAVID

For some strange reason this boy named David was popular in the first grade. But once we hit second grade, it was all over for this poor little kid, who actually ended up being quite geeky. He had a very thick head of dark brown hair which seemed to thicken more and more each year. There were cowlicks all over his head and he never quite perfected a hairstyle that worked for him.

This only got worse over time. He was chubby with chewed nails that left his hands wet and nasty. Ironically, having chewed nails is one of my biggest turn-offs today. Apparently in the first grade it hadn't become a deal breaker yet. He was a nice Jewish boy; in fact, this was the only Jewish boy I ever had a crush on. Mom and Nana would have been thrilled! But back in those days I never in a million years would have shared my crush with them or anyone else except Kara.

Kara was my best friend from first grade all the way through high school. There were many good and bad memories about Kara which I will share throughout this book. She was an adorable, chunky child with straggly long dark hair. She had teeth that were so crooked I used to wonder if braces could actually help her. Eventually braces did wonders for Kara's smile. But it didn't help her through all the years at Gibbons Elementary School.

I, on the other hand, was tall and thin with long, thick blonde hair. I got my ears pierced that year and inherited some cute clothes from my older sister, Stacey. First grade was a good year for me. When I look back at that class picture I would have to say that it may have been my cutest year, not counting today, of course!

But David only wanted Kara. Kara was always able to pull off anything she wanted. Later in life and post-braces, Kara was very cute. But I didn't get what was so appealing about her back then. Even in first grade, Kara had this confident attitude that would always get her what she wanted. Kara was artist of the week, gerbil babysitter over the school vacations and the one girl that David had a crush on. Back then, I had a defeatist attitude – I knew he would like Kara over me.

I grew to expect that good things came her way and that I would just be in her shadow. This is the earliest that I can pinpoint myself having such negative beliefs. As an insecure 6-year-old girl, I had no idea that my negative beliefs were creating the negative outcomes in my life. A concept I wasn't going to believe until I transformed my life in my early 30s.

So what do you do if you have these negative beliefs?

If you feel like you are in the shadow of a friend, believe you will never find love or are always envious of others' lives, then it is high time you change your beliefs. So many people neglect to understand that our thoughts are just mere beliefs that we create. And not only do we have power over creating our beliefs, but we can make a choice not to believe them. Sure, Kara may have had a different upbringing and many different factors and influences that gave her the confidence to believe good things would come her way. Kara and I had no clue that this was even happening, as we were both so young.

As adults we need to get a better grip on the messages we repeat over and over again in our heads. If you keep repeating that true love will never happen for you, then you are setting yourself up for failure in the romance department. Change the chatter in your head. Repeat positive affirmations like "I will find true love" and "I am lovable" and "I deserve happiness." Because you will, you are, and you do.

Can changing your beliefs really change your life?

We do have the power to make drastic changes in our lives by simply changing our thoughts. I find it very frustrating when people I meet are so lazy that they refuse to even give it a shot. I mean, realistically, do you actually believe that there is some higher power out there forcing you to have negative thoughts? Is someone holding you hostage and telling you that you must think your life is miserable and hopeless? This is not the case at all. Most of our beliefs come from messages we learned as children - and we never even recognized that these messages were becoming our core beliefs. It is never too late to create new beliefs. I am not saying that by just changing your thoughts you will automatically find true love, but I *can* say that if you continue to be a miserable pessimist your chances are a lot lower.

Recently I hosted a group activity with single women who were looking for healthy relationships. I asked each of the women to use a scale between one and five to rank how likely they believe they will find love. A five would symbolize that they were confident that they would find this, and a one indicated that they believed they would never find true love. I told the women that I was sure that anyone who put a five down next to this question was more likely to reach their goal. I watched each woman in the group pick up their pen and change the number to a five.

Now just writing the number five down on a piece of paper was no guarantee, but it was a first step in the right direction. And I can't promise that all the fives will live happily ever after but I can assure you that those ones will be single a lot longer.

So in a nutshell what exactly should I be doing?

When you find yourself convincing yourself that life is miserable and you are destined to be lonely or unhappy forever, you need to replace those thoughts. Some people find it easier to distract themselves by having a drink, smoking a cigarette or taking a pill when they start feeling so helpless. This will never solve the problem. You need to be proactive and take a look at the exercises described in chapter 14. Please be open to the possibilities - as you will see by the end of this book, it completely transformed my life.

3 - RONNIE

His name was Ronnie and we were in 5th grade. He was kind of a skinny, scrawnier kid back in those days but with a face as cute as a button. He had straight brown hair, brown eyes and a great Italian complexion. His facial features were completely adorable. He seemed to know he was the cutest kid in the fifth grade. And if he had any doubts, his very popular girlfriend was always there to remind him.

I, on the other hand, was on the fast track to losing my cuteness. Fifth grade was the year my nose broke for the first time. My sister Stacey and I were playing softball and I got hit right in the center of my face and broke my nose. The doctor said I needed to continue growing before they could fix it properly. My nose, along with weighing in at a mere 40 pounds and being taller than anyone in my class was not exactly making me popular. I was ready for braces but had two years to go before the orthodontist agreed. On top of that I was having a bad year and often made the "tsss" sound with my tongue when I was annoyed. This was a sound that led to more tormenting than I care to remember.

Back to Ronnie and Millie, who were the most popular couple at the Gibbons Elementary School in Stoughton, MA that year. I was never quite sure what made Millie so popular. Honestly, she was a bit overweight, had acne and boobs. Oh yes, that was it! Millie was the first girl at Gibbons School to hit puberty and even in the fifth grade this would get you noticed.

I wanted to be popular like Millie and tried to emulate her. I distinctly remember not washing my face hoping I would develop acne to look more like her. It never exactly worked as I happen to have some great genes as far as skin goes. Perhaps if I just stuffed some socks in my bra it may have been easier. But that would require me to have a bra and back then my body wasn't even close to needing any support. In fact even today my body doesn't require too much support.

But it wasn't just her boobs. Millie had this abundance of confidence. She came from a big popular family and each and every sibling seemed to have a free pass to the popular club just for having the last name. On the other hand, I lacked confidence and was so shy and never even had the guts to talk to Ronnie.

So what should I do if I am shy or insecure?

Never try and copy someone else. In order to ever become cool or popular you need to be yourself. By the way, "be yourself" is the worst advice and a bit of advice I will never dish out to any of my shy or insecure single clients. Someone that is shy and insecure has trouble defining who they really are. When they hear the expression "be yourself" they walk away thinking, who is going to like my insecure, shy self?

So if you are shy or insecure I have some advice to help you through it. If only I had these tips back in the days of Gibbons School I could actually have spoken to Ronnie. First tip is to practice in the mirror. I know it seems ridiculous to actually do this but don't worry - no one is watching, except for you. Stand in front of that mirror and rehearse your first five minutes of a conversation with the person you want to pursue. Pretend you are confident, smile, make eye contact and small jokes, ask your date questions and give responses. Do this activity five minutes a night and I can assure you that it will help you in the dating world. It might look like this: "Hey, Ronnie how is that book report working out for you?" Or "Hey Ronnie nice job knocking me over with the dodge ball in gym class." Or even, "Ronnie what the heck do you see in Millie anyway?"

What if I still have trouble walking up to someone like Ronnie?

These days, there are so many easy ways to meet singles, if you don't want to attempt a conversation in gym class or at a bar. Internet dating is a very popular alterative, and you can start your conversations virtually, which many people find much less intimidating. You can spend hours thinking of how to craft the response and no one would ever even know. Sure, there is a lot of rejection involved in Internet dating and it may be quite time consuming, but view it as practice. The more emails you craft and deliver the better you will get at this.

I remember my son doing a school project on baseball. He quoted Babe Ruth as saying, "every strike brings me closer to the next home run." This applies perfectly to both baseball and dating.

I own my own speed dating company and think it is another terrific way to practice starting up those initial conversations. Here you have the chance to participate in multiple five-minute dates with a variety of other singles. Your best bet is to try and make your first date be with someone you are not attracted to. I know it sounds mean, but a practice date is always helpful. And don't feel so bad -

just because you are not attracted to him doesn't mean that no one else will be. All that practicing you have been doing in the mirror can now be orchestrated at the speed dating event.

These are great suggestions, but this is a hard thing to overcome, any other suggestions?

Yes plenty of them...

Imagine you are with your brother or your best friend. If the guy you are with is intimidating you in any way, just imagine the face of someone you are close to and act the natural way that you would act in front of that person. Be careful with this tip, however, as you don't want to call him by the wrong name. That could lead to a variety of other problems, especially if you call someone by your brother's name. Now that could be creepy! But my point is that we are most comfortable in front of those we are closest to. So if you feel confused or unsure about what "being yourself" should really look like, imagining your behavior with familiar friends and family members will guide you there.

It is usually not *what* you are saying that your date is paying attention to but more so *how* you are saying it. In other words, if the date is really into you, you could almost say anything as long as you say it with confidence. But when your date is annoyed you could say the exact same thing and be completely ruined. So don't analyze everything you are saying. Just pretend to be confident and I can tell you that your date will find whatever you are talking about that much more appealing.

My last tip on this subject is to fake it. Women are notorious for faking orgasms - surely this has got to be a little easier! Having hosted hundreds of speed dating events I can tell you that the way one walks into the event tells quite a bit about the person. I have seen speed daters enter the room looking down, with their hands in their pockets. When I approach them they mumble a shy hello and never actually look at me. Their posture is poor and they never even take their coat off. Many think everything is about physical appearance, and of course to some degree this is true. But I have seen many average-looking people walk in the room with a big smile and a great attitude. These are the women and the men that make the most matches at the speed dating events. So even if you are feeling insecure, just pretend to be confident! With good posture and a smile you are well on your way.

So in a nutshell, what exactly should I be doing?

You should practice the things we discussed above every day. It is just like playing a sport or musical instrument. Although some are naturals, others need to put a little more effort into it. And always remember that everyone is a little insecure! So if you are on a date with someone that is really good looking, has a highly successful career or is well travelled, don't be fooled. There is still a real person under all that pizzazz and you have no reason to be intimidated. Just remind yourself that you too are great and this person is lucky to be with such a terrific catch. I don't care if you are a doctor or a lawyer or once backpacked through Europe. It is about the person that you are inside, and this guy is lucky to be with you.

4 - MICHAEL

There were three Michaels that hung around my house on Winslow Drive in Stoughton, Massachusetts. They swam at our pool, came to our parties and flirted with my mother. I think they were actually more interested in my mom than anything, but that didn't stop me from wanting their attention. The Michael I liked most lived right in the neighborhood. This crush lasted 10 years - an entire decade! Michael would go for early morning walks carrying this giant boom box, blaring bands like Def Leppard and AC/DC. I was frequently woken by his loud music on those hot summer mornings. I'd jump up and run straight for my window.

There he was in a form fitting t-shirt, baseball cap and swimming trunks. My heart would hit the floor and the butterflies felt more like bats in my stomach. Michael was positively gorgeous. He had a great face with chiseled features, thick, dark hair and a bronze tan that seemed to last all the way through the winter months. His face was beautiful, but it was Michael's body that turned everyone's heads. For a young teenager his muscles were out of control. You would even hear the adults talking about how Michael should be a movie star.

Now my pre-teen years weren't the most appealing for me. I was skinny as a pencil and always had a pair of pink nose plugs hanging around my neck. It would have been a whole lot cooler to just hold my nose than to clip this pink rubber to the center of my face when jumping in the water. Michael used to jokingly ask me why I had bubble gum on my nose, but I never caught on. I also got braces, my hair grew long but was kind of unmanageable and I still didn't have any boobs or curves.

Michael and I were together all of the time. He was the first one in my pool most mornings. My family vacationed at his family cottage in Martha's Vineyard. I would share a bunk bed with his sister in the very next room. We went to school together, played at each other's houses and once I hit about 12 and Michael was 14 our parents would all go out and leave the four of us siblings together while they enjoyed dinner, a movie or perhaps even a party. We would have our own sort of party. And as long as Michael was with me, our parents could stay out all night for all I cared.

I woke up one morning at about age 12 to the phone ringing. I answered it and it was Michael in my basement calling us from the other line. For some reason it seemed funny that Michael would sneak in my house and pull pranks. I was always prepared for Michael's surprise visits. I kept a cool halter top and jeans lying out on my dresser so I could quickly get dressed and look hot for my all-time favorite crush. He would come up from the basement and eat pop tarts with me, watch TV, and always end up in our swimming pool.

On one of our trips to the Vineyard cottage, Michael and I took the canoe out. I was wearing a blue and pink one-piece bathing suit with my ever-present nose plugs around my neck. Michael was wearing a bathing suit and no shirt to expose his muscles. We took the canoe way past our destination and Michael pulled out the fishing rod. I was really hoping he would kiss me on that hot summer day. I pretended to relax and soak up the sun while he sat with his fishing rod in water. I played it cool but tried to look appealing as I lied back and relaxed. Michael was paying more attention to that damn fishing rod. I waited and waited. Michael started to reel his line in and I thought he was ready to put it away. Nope, he had a fish and was so proud. He took it off the hook and let it flop around inside of the canoe. I was very freaked out by this slimy creature and I screamed like a lunatic. Michael was so annoyed he threw the fish back in the water and quickly rowed us back to shore. Not a single kiss!

Later that same day we jumped the waves together at South Beach. These waves were enormous and could pull you under the water with just a moment's notice. It was adventurous and fun! I wasn't afraid of the waves and thought this was a good chance to redeem myself from the fish incident. Michael and I laughed and stayed in that water for hours. Sometimes the waves would push us into each other and our adolescent bodies would touch. We would jump away from each other and just laugh it all off. Meanwhile my 13-year-old body began feeling things it had never felt before. Michael would pick me up sometimes and throw my skinny body down into the water with a splash. This was the most he ever touched me on these trips to his summer hot spot. We had a blast, but that longed-for kiss seemed to be miles away!

There were times when my crush on Michael was less intense than others but I never gave up wanting that kiss. We became great friends over the years. As kids it was riding bikes, swimming, birthday parties and kickball games.

We drifted a little during high school but met up again in college. Michael and I both went to Southeastern Massachusetts University (SMU) and our friendship continued. He was in a relationship with a girl we knew from back home. One time Michael called me and asked me for help. His girlfriend broke up with him and Michael was crushed. He came to my off-campus house and asked me what he should do. I actually called his girlfriend and convinced her to go back out with him. In the back of my head I hoped this was finally my time to get that kiss from Michael. But his girlfriend quickly forgave him and I was still stuck in the friend zone.

The next year he invited my roommate, Yvonne, and I over to his off-campus house. I was still holding on to a little spark of hope. I told Yvonne we were nothing more than good friends and she believed it. In fact, she believed it so much that the two of them ended up making out and going into his room for their own private party. I was left with his roommate. He was a spiky-haired, short blonde kid who I barely remember. We kissed for a while and he brought me into his bedroom. I lied on his bed closed my eyes tight and pretended he was Michael. Even with the four beers I drank, I couldn't fantasize that well. We kissed a little longer and both fell asleep. I slipped away before he woke up, grabbed Yvonne and went back home. That night ended but Yvonne continued to have a brief fling with Michael. I pretended to be happy for her and never told either one of them that it was tearing me up inside.

During our senior year at SMU, Michael and I were at the same party once again. I knew I was looking the best I possibly could. I had a new pair of Jordache jeans on and a pink Champion sweatshirt. My roommates Chrissy and Lori helped me to do my hair that night and I thought I finally looked as cool as they did. Still my roommates had no idea

I had a crush on Michael. I always made sure everyone saw us as buddies from back home.

Michael showed up at the party, walked up to me and told me I looked hot. He even put his hand on my hip and said that my new jeans looked very sexy on me. He and I flirted and it seemed a little more intense than normal. I knew we would be graduating soon and didn't want to miss any opportunities to be with him. We joked around about how this could finally be our night together after all of our years of being just buddies. He said he just might show up at my house at 1:00 a.m. to close the deal. He must have been able to sense that I was interested but I couldn't tell if he was or perhaps he was just being funny and cute. I went back to my house by 12:30 a.m. and lied on my bed. I waited and waited. I watched the clock turn to 1:00 a.m. and fell asleep. Michael never came over that night. We graduated and went our separate ways. It has been 20 years, and I haven't seen Michael since.

Michael and I were trapped in the friend zone, which is a great place to be if all you are looking for is a friendship. But as you can see, I spent years and years yearning for us to become more than friends. I looked back many times and thought, if only I told him what I was feeling!

Isn't there a risk of losing the friendship if you tell your crush how you are really feeling?

Yes, of course there is a risk of losing the friendship if you decide to let that special person know how you really feel. But in almost every case, a platonic friendship is going to end when one party in the couple does find true love. When I met my husband Erik, one of his best friends was a girl. He warned me about this and hoped I could accept it. She was a great girl and I was not threatened by the friendship whatsoever. Her name was Jesse and I met her many times. They never flirted but they had a great chemistry and both always welcomed me into the relationship. Jesse met us in Las Vegas and witnessed our marriage. She also got married and started her own family. As time passed, Jesse and Erik just lost touch. In most cases this is just what happens in life. So the first step is to let go of the fear of losing the friendship because you will likely lose it anyways.

So after we take your advice and tell them how we feel, what should we do next?

After you come clean and tell them the truth about how you feel, it is time to stop being their best friend. Don't be so available every time they have a relationship problem or reach out to you for emotional support. Let them find a new best friend and remove yourself from this role.

Next you need to start dating and let this person see you as a sexy and datable single. I had a couple attend a speed dating event two years ago. Heather and Dave were neighbors, both recently divorced and great friends. They came to one of my speed dating events together and selected each other as a potential match. They have been dating ever since. By witnessing each other at the event going on mini-dates with several people each, they saw each other in a different light. In order to move out of the friend zone you need to show this person how desirable you are to other singles.

Ask that person out on a date. And be sure to use the word date in your proposal. Don't waste time asking them to go to dinner or grab a movie because it will just be interpreted as a friendship. Once you are on that date you need to act the part of a potential partner. You want to compliment this person, make eye contact and physically touch them. And no I don't mean stuff your hand between their legs under the dinner table! I simply mean to touch their back as you follow them into the restaurant, put your hand on their hand when you are in conversation or even flirtatiously hit their arm when joking around.

So in a nutshell what exactly should I be doing?

Don't be afraid of losing the friendship or of potentially getting rejected. If it doesn't work out you will now be in a place to find everything you want in a relationship. You won't have to wait around anymore hoping that your best friend will finally turn into your lover. You won't be left wondering if this boy will ever kiss you while jumping through the waves at South Beach on Martha's Vineyard.

5 - NICK

Tenth grade was the year it all changed for me. I discovered partying and became especially enticed by vodka, which today just the smell of, could make me want to vomit. I also had a whole new look by this time. Big hair was in style and this worked for me as I had thicker hair than anyone I knew. I used a lot of Aqua Net hair spray to make my bleached blonde 'do look even bigger than it really was. I loved wearing concert t-shirts with jeans that we used to call bubble gum jeans. These jeans were skintight and I was lucky enough to be a size four, so I could pull this look off quite well. I wore lots of eye shadow and mascara back in those days too. I learned from a makeup artist at Jordan Marsh in the Westgate Mall that if I wore a lot of eye makeup it would take the focus away from my still-crooked nose.

My parents kept a full bar right in the den and it was loaded with vodka. Joyce, Kara and I would mix ourselves a couple of drinks, add some water to the bottle so my parents wouldn't notice, and take off into the woods to meet some friends for a night of partying.

Initially, I had a boy named Neil on my mind as we walked a half-mile into woods to meet up with our friends. But Neil was quite popular with the ladies and this particular night, it was easier to grab the attention of his best friend Nick. Nick was cute with his wavy black hair, light complexion and small Irish facial features. He was a bit taller than me and wore a very appealing black leather jacket. Nick was also 3 years older than me.

Nick and I continued to drink, laugh and flirt until the party started to break up. By this point, I was well on my way to being intoxicated. Nick was a true gentleman and offered to walk me home. I have no idea what happened to Joyce and Kara at this point in the night. It didn't matter because I was drunk and only cared where Nick was. We reached my house and made a cozy spot in the woods behind the picket fence. I sat on Nick's leather jacket, we made out and Nick was the first boy to ever touch me under my clothes. I was drunk as could be and started feeling queasy, but didn't want Nick to leave. It was getting very cold and my curfew was just minutes away. We stood up, Nick put his jacket on me and we jumped the fence, landing in my back yard patio. I picked up the outdoor telephone to call my parents and tell them I was running late and would be home soon. My dad was able to hear us through an open window and abruptly appeared at the back door. Nick took one look at my dad, quickly jumped the fence and ran 80 miles an hour down the street.

I woke up the next morning with my first real hangover. I was still wearing my clothes, including Nick's leather jacket. I thought for sure he had to call me or stop by to retrieve it. But he never did! His brother was in my grade and when I saw him at school on Monday, he asked me to return it to him. I brought it to school on Tuesday and was afraid I would never be with Nick again.

The next weekend Joyce, Kara and I returned to our party spot in the woods with our now watered down vodka drinks. Nick greeted me with a smile as if he'd been waiting for me. Back in those days we used the term scooping to define what Nick and I were doing. To me this basically meant that we would make out and experiment with some touching. To others it meant having sex. Nick and I scooped on each other weekend after weekend. Nick never called me during the week, we never saw each other in between parties, yet I still was willing to scoop on my new found crush week after week.

That winter my parents went away for the weekend and my sister and I decided to have a party. Kind of a stupid idea, but we were teenagers and always up for some fun. She was in twelfth grade, and together we spread the word about our little bash. Nick showed up and I had hoped the scooping relationship would continue. I walked down to our basement and caught him making out with Bethany, one of my trashier friends. I stormed away in complete disgust. To add fuel to the fire, Bethany came after me and told me that Nick said "she was more like a woman and I was more like a girl." That was the end of my relationship with Nick.

So what exactly did he mean by that woman/girl comment?

Bethany had a bit of a reputation with the guys, if you know what I mean. The truth is, I was still a virgin at that time, and although I liked being touched by Nick, I knew that my first sexual encounter was going to be with someone that was really into me. And we all know Nick was obviously not that guy. I will leave the details of what happened between Bethany and Nick to your imagination.

Why is it that he wanted to scoop on you at these parties, yet never called you?

Nick was getting exactly what he wanted, a cute girl to hook up with on the weekends. He didn't want any commitment from the drunk, party girl that I was. He just wanted a hook up. I basically gave him permission to do just that. He learned very quickly that I was willing to accept the situation for exactly what it was, with no demands put on him. I don't blame Nick at all for this. After all, what teenaged boy wouldn't like that arrangement?

I often hear women today say that they want more of a commitment from the men they are dating, but they are afraid to ask for this because they fear that it will make them appear needy and perhaps drive the guy away.

If you are casually dating someone and want a commitment, then you need to ask for that. The easiest time to do this is prior to having a sexual relationship. I realize that for some of you, this advice may be a bit too late.

Don't be afraid to ask for what you want. If you are willing to accept casual sex from a partner and not ask for anything more, then you are sending out a powerful message. You are telling him that this is the type of relationship you feel you are worthy of. Let him know, as soon as possible, that you are a respectable woman and do not want to be trapped in a sexual relationship with someone that isn't willing to commit to you. I can assure you that the guy you are with is either going to respect you more and be willing to commit or it was never going to lead to the relationship you were hoping for. It is always better to find this out sooner than later.

So in a nutshell what should I learn from this crush?

There is nothing cute about drinking so much vodka that you can barely stand up straight. If you want a guy to like you for more than just a scoop or hook up, then you have to have some respect for yourself and avoid the abuse of alcohol.

Now, Bethany wasn't any smarter than me. She may have thought she was a "woman" that night, but Nick never called her either. Having sex too quickly with someone may entice them initially, but in most cases you will wake up the next morning and do the walk of shame. Show some self-respect and keep your clothes on until you know that your partner is committed to you. You never want to lead a guy into thinking you have such little dignity that one-night stands and sleazy hook ups will suffice, unless a one night stand is all that you are looking for.

If you have made some mistakes in the past don't waste energy feeling shamed and embarrassed, just learn from these mistakes and move on. It is never too late to make some healthy changes in your love life.

6 - JOEY

So we all wanted that bad boy at one point in time. OK fine - I wanted him most of the time. Joey was my first super-cool boyfriend. I really don't know if I ever liked him all that much; I just thought he ranked very high on the cool scale and that if I dated him I would push my own rank up a bit.

It was the night of our party and I had just stormed away from Nick and Bethany. I was both upset and annoyed by the situation. Moments later Joey showed up to the party looking rather cute. I didn't really know him personally but he was friends with my friend Ted. Joey was blonde-haired, blue-eyed and a bit on the short, stocky side. He had a pale complexion without a whole lot of character to his plain face. I think I had him by an inch, but if I stuck my hip out we were about even.

I thought Joey was pretty cool, and I was excited and flattered that he instantly showed an interest in me. Joey had a brilliant idea to take our friend Ted and I out for a joy ride. So I actually left my own party to go on this little adventure with Joey and Ted. Did I mention he didn't have a driver's license, had his mother's stolen car and had more than a few beers to drink at the party? Sure enough he crashed the car.

I didn't get hurt but Ted did, and we spent a good hour or two in the emergency room at the Goddard Hospital, where my Mom was employed as a nurse. Good thing no one recognized me. My mother would have been quite embarrassed to hear that I was in the emergency room with two drunken boys. Joey and I cruised around on wheel chairs while we waited for Ted to be released with a neck brace. Amazingly we never got caught for any of this. Back to the party we went, and I spent the rest of the night hanging out with my new and first real boyfriend.

We went to parties together, drank, smoked pot and had sex. Joey was my very first sexual experience. It was uneventful, to be honest. My Dad dropped me off at his house so Joey and I could watch a movie. Today we call that "a movie date without the movie." Joey lived in a cape with two bedrooms upstairs and two downstairs. One of the downstairs bedrooms was used as a TV room and that is where we pretended to watch a movie. My sister and I had secretly viewed a bunch of our parents' pornography tapes, so I thought this was going to be some over-the-top experience.

It was not even close. Joey uncrossed my legs and removed my clothes as if he was taking a dress off of a Barbie doll. Then he quickly removed his pants and sex lasted for under 60 seconds. When we were done I called my dad and went home. He asked me how the movie was and I replied that it was fine. We drove the rest of the way in silence and my dad had no idea that his daughter had just lost her virginity. I was now one of the tenth grade girls having sex and I thought that was a good thing.

Joey and I were into each other for a few months. I didn't know much about having a boyfriend, but he had a car and our best friends (Kara and Ted) were dating too, so this felt like the right thing to do. A few months into it Joey disappeared. Literally, this 16-year-old kid seemed to fall off the small planet of Stoughton, Massachusetts. His friends told me that last they knew he went to Harlem, New York to buy some weed. So I waited and waited.

One day, while sitting in my boring science class, I spotted my high school dropout of a boyfriend peeking through the small rectangular glass window of the science room door. I was so excited to see him again after three long weeks! I asked my teacher if I could use the bathroom pass. I took the pass and walked straight out of the building to go hang out with Joey for the rest of the day.

We dragged this on for another month or two. Then Joey sprung the big news on me. He was going away for a long time. Joey told me he was going to live with his father in Florida because he was getting in too much trouble around here. Others said it was a cover story and he was off to a juvenile detention center. I never really found out the truth but secretly I was happy to say goodbye. Through Joey I had met a lot of other cute and very cool boys that I wanted to hang out with. I was getting tired of being Joey's girlfriend and ready to have some fun. Joey and I shed some tears and said our goodbyes. We never clarified if we were breaking up, would still call each other, or write letters. It was just a kiss and a hug and my first boyfriend was gone.

So what is so bad about liking bad boys anyways?

Bad boys never stick around. Whether they cheat, move away or get sent to a juvenile detention center it is going to end somehow - they are basically jerks. I am not saying Joey was *exactly* a jerk. He just conveniently led me to the topic of bad boys. They are typically emotionally unavailable, they are known to disrespect women and think primarily of themselves. They can also be selfish, arrogant and thugs. They have a way of manipulating women and are quite proud of this talent. It's amazing how many women out there are willing to tolerate this abuse. Yes, they seem cool because they often like fast cars, smoke cigarettes, have tattoos, party, gamble, have criminal histories and participate in many other self-destructive, unhealthy habits. But trust me – they are not cool.

What should we do if we find this type of guy sexy?

I want all women to understand something. You can find a guy with a bit of an edge to him that doesn't possess the manipulating and abusive traits that these bad boys have. So from now on let's start saying that we like a guy with an edge and avoid the abusive criminals that women with high self-esteems like ourselves should never entertain.

I met a guy who perfectly fits this description. I will talk more about that crush in a later chapter. But he was cool and had an edge. He had a Pitbull, played hockey, loved poker and even had a motorcycle. This was the kind of guy I felt safe with. I could walk down a dark alley with him and know he could protect me. Most women want a man that makes them feel safe and has the characteristics that make them tough and manly.

But let me tell you, this guy was not abusive, he never tried to manipulate me or embarrass me. He could engage in a deep conversation and was emotionally available. There were no wife beater shirts or criminal records either. My point is to stop convincing yourself that the "bad boys" are sexy and the "good boys" are boring and lame. Anyone that believes this is just plain ridiculous.

So, in a nutshell, what should we do if we are constantly attracted to these bad boys?

If you always end up with a man that abuses and mistreats you then you need to take a close hard look at yourself! Perhaps this is familiar to you. Were you ignored and disrespected by your father and you chose to recreate this? Do you believe that you are not worthy of being respected and loved by a man? Do you have such little dignity and self-respect that you think this is acceptable? It doesn't really matter how you answer any of these questions. I just hope at some point you will wake up and realize that "bad boys" are complete losers that will never love and respect you. A guy with an edge is cool and sexy and will be able to love and respect you. It is up to you to decide what you think you deserve.

7 - JIMMY

Right after Joey left I couldn't wait to start checking out other guys. OK, the truth is even before Joey left, I always had my eye on one particular guy! He was that one boy that I couldn't seem to get out of my head all through high school. Allow me to paint a picture of Jimmy. He was tall with dark wavy hair. I can see him walking down the hallway at Stoughton High School wearing black Levi corduroys and an off-white velour shirt with a collar and two buttons at the top and tan work boots. Those boots were the style back then and any guy sporting them automatically appeared to be cool. He had a great complexion, big brown eyes and a very cute smirk which was the closest thing to a smile that he ever actually gave me.

Jimmy only seemed to notice I was alive after many beers at a Quality Steel party. Quality Steel was a business buried in an industrial area that was nestled in the woods. It was a perfect spot for a bunch of young, under-aged drinkers to chip in for a keg and party. Sometimes 50 or so of us would stand out there by a fire and drink for hours.

I used to go every weekend with my best and only friends, Joyce and Kara. We all had a guy in mind when we ventured off with our two dollars for a refillable keg cup. Kara was always thinking about a kid named Derek who was a grade behind us. Joyce was usually chasing after one of Jimmy's brothers, of which he had many. I was pretty loyal to finding Jimmy weekend after weekend. He drove a sporty white car and his best friend drove a red one with a white roof. Both were very recognizable and either one usually escorted Jimmy to the party.

My heart would begin racing as I strategized how to get his attention. Basically, I had no clue. And truth is, I can barely remember how it ever played out. I was always a little drunk and the only parts I remember were Jimmy and I ending up in the back seat of someone's car. I don't think we ever said two words to each other. OK maybe *two* words, but the rest consisted of making out in the back seat of a car that smelled like leather, beer and cigarettes.

Jimmy and I scooped on each other multiple times between my sophomore and senior year of high school. I loved being with him but had enough morals to know better than to take my clothes off and have sex in the back of his buddy's car. My mother always put the fear of sexually transmitted diseases and unplanned pregnancies in my head starting in middle school. Whether or not it was her intention, it saved me from the reputation of being a slut. One that some of my friends acquired quite quickly. I knew having sex with Jimmy wasn't the way to turn him into my boyfriend, but I had no idea what it would actually take to do this.

I received one and only one phone call from Jimmy during our entire three years of hooking up. The phone rang at about 5:00 on a Saturday evening the day after Jimmy and I made out on the hood of his friend's car at the

Quality Steel party. There was no caller ID in those days so I had no clue who would be on the other end of the phone until I said hello. Jimmy was on the other end and asked me what I was up to. My heart started racing 100 miles an hour and I felt so nervous. I didn't even have a clue how to play it cool. I mouthed to my sister that it was Jimmy. She whispered some quick advice to me and suggested I invite him to come to Wendy's with us for dinner. So I trusted Stacey had more experience than I did with a guy calling and invited Jimmy to come along. Jimmy quickly declined and said he had to go. Talk about availability- the guy calls once and I ask him to hang out that very minute. Only one of the many big mistakes I made with Jimmy. It turns out that Stacey was just as clueless as I was.

"If I only knew then what I know now" is the perfect expression to describe what might have worked with Jimmy. The number one lesson learned is to not be so available. We hear this all of the time. But I wanted a boyfriend and Jimmy was one that I would have done just about anything for. So how could I skip a Quality Steel party when I knew that chances were I would get to make out and hook up with the hottest guy in Stoughton (which isn't saying a whole lot)? Well if I never showed up perhaps Jimmy would have wondered where I was. But in reality I doubt it. I think in this case out of sight was out of mind.

So what could you have done differently to get Jimmy's attention?

Well here is an idea...

I show up to the party looking as hot as one can in layers of warm clothing to help me survive these cold nights. I have a couple of beers, talk to a few people and say a quick hello to Jimmy and head out. Gather my friends and have something better to do. Perhaps we could have left and grabbed a pizza at Town Spa or a movie at the Stoughton Cinema. But we never did. We stayed until our 1:00 AM curfew (which now seems awfully late for a 15-year-old party girl). Joyce, Kara and I almost never left together unless Joyce was in the front seat with one of Jimmy's brothers. We were all so available to the guys we had crushes on.

What if all of your friends want to stay at the party? Should you really be forced to leave just to make a statement to Jimmy?

There is another angle I could have taken. Jimmy was always hanging out with a group of friends. Instead of walking up and saying hello to Jimmy directly, I could have tried to win the friends over first. Walk up and make a joke and chat up his buddies, who, by the way, were all very cute! A cool move may include me turning my head toward Jimmy for a quick hello and then back to the crowd. After a few minutes I would say bye to the crowd of friends and regroup with Joyce and Kara. Again, I can't guarantee this would have made much of a difference for a couple of teenagers, but I highly suggest you give this a shot when you are in a bar, at a club, party or other social function.

So, in a nutshell, what exactly should I be doing?

Don't be so available. I don't exactly mean physically available. If a guy doesn't give you three days notice for a date and you are free and want to go then fine, go for it! But in general you need to get a life and be genuinely unavailable. I know the last thing you want me to do is start rambling off a list of potential hobbies. But the truth is, if you are newly dating someone and he knows you have volleyball every Tuesday and Thursday night, he will make an effort to clear his schedule on Wednesdays if he really wants to see you. He is never going to think you are a great girl, but because you are not free on Tuesday and Thursday nights he needs to dump you. In fact, that will just entice him more.

When one or both of you have children, coordinating times can be a real challenge. But don't always be the one to offer to change your schedule to accommodate him, especially if you are newly dating. It should be a shared effort. And when you both really like each other, you will put the extra effort forth to fit in quality time together. And when you are not available, it might just entice him even more to plan ahead and be sure that he can be available to see you when you are free. Being available and waiting seven nights a week will make you less appealing. So please get a life, find a hobby and enjoy your time with your children! This is what will make the guy find you more attractive.

8 - VINNIE

Vinnie was the first guy I dated after high school. He was five years older than me. Vinnie was just about my height with black hair, green eyes and that big Italian nose. Five years earlier he won most popular in his High School yearbook, and for some reason I thought this was still a redeeming quality a half-decade later.

I still had my big bleached blonde hair, but this particular day I was wearing a sexy little flowered bikini and hoping to get the attention of someone that could become my next boyfriend.

It was late May in 1987, and Vinnie showed up to our famous Memorial Day weekend bash. We had a great in-ground swimming pool and my parents were very cool with us hosting an annual Memorial Day party. My parents would throw a bunch of hot dogs and hamburgers on the grill and we would pick up a keg of beer. There was also a hot tub in the basement and whatever folks stuck around late enough could have a dip in there, too.

Vinnie showed an interest in me right away. I guess the bikini was doing the trick. I took a ride in his charcoal brown Camaro (still wearing my bikini), returned to the party, we smoked a joint together and landed in the hot tub by midnight. This was the start of an exciting new relationship.

I was 18 and he was 23. He could buy alcohol without a problem, had lots of cool friends, a fast sports car that we tooled around in and life was fun for a while. The honeymoon period lasted for about three months. I was proud to be his new girlfriend, went to all of his softball games and we hit some fancy restaurants. But after three months, I started to realize that this wasn't what I had signed up for.

Vinnie was my first emotionally, physically and sexually abusive boyfriend. It started off slow, and I really didn't realize how bad it got until I was two years deep into an abusive, unhealthy relationship in which I felt trapped.

Vinnie wanted to have sex multiple times a day. I had only had sex a handful of times in my life and had not even figured out what pleasured me. I was having sex to please the men and sacrificed my own pleasure every time. This wasn't so bad as it was very infrequent in the past. But with Vinnie he had his own apartment and expected a whole lot more from me. Intercourse hurt and he had no regard for my complaints. In fact Vinnie would actually withdraw any physical contact with me for days if I ever denied him sex. He once rationalized that if I wouldn't give him oral sex for the tenth time that day than he wouldn't hold me. At 18, this actually made sense to me.

Vinnie physically pushed me, threw things at me and called me every harassing name you can imagine. I hated to be anywhere near him but felt trapped. I went away to college that year and came home every weekend to spend it with this man. Can you imagine the great years of college that I sacrificed for this unhealthy relationship? I was afraid to end it for two reasons. First, I knew how angry he would become as he gained great pleasure out of controlling me. Second, I was afraid that no one else would ever love me.

I came home every weekend from college because Vinnie would have become mean and jealous if I didn't. And I felt that I would be responsible for his actions. Seems insane as I look back on those days, but that is exactly what was happening. When we were at a party Vinnie would get jealous if I was talking to another guy. He would mouth words like whore and bitch to me so that only I would see it happening. Instead of dumping Vinnie, I would just avoid talking to any other guys. Forget my desire to have fun and make new friends. It became my job to keep Vinnie happy and avoid any situation that might upset him.

One night we were supposed to meet at our mutual friend's party. I showed up early and stayed for about three hours. Vinnie never arrived. I was upset and unable to have any fun. I worried that I had done something to anger him. After I left he showed up and my sister casually told him I had been looking for him. For some reason this enraged Vinnie. He went home and called me, claiming my sister was a variety of things even worse than a whore and a bitch. He said if I didn't come over immediately he would call on my parents' line and leave them a message telling them what my sister was. I jumped in my car, drove to his house, ran in and pulled the mouthpiece of Vinnie's only phone off of the cradle. I ran to my car before he could get to me and drove home with the mouth piece in my hand. It was a scary thing to do but less scary than imagining him calling my parents. So I took the risk and by the next morning he had calmed down.

One rare night I had plans with Joyce and Kara. Vinnie asked to take me to dinner prior to my girl's night out. I was a college student and never turned down a free meal. Plus I had hoped this meant that Vinnie wasn't angry with me and just wanted us to spend some time together early that evening. We went to a cute little restaurant in Stoughton Center and from the minute we arrived, Vinnie harassed me. He brought up every incident when I spoke to another guy, accused me of cheating on him and called me every name imaginable. I sat there in silence and listened to all of the abuse. I imagined getting up and running to a pay phone to call my dad. I knew my dad would pick me up with no questions asked and I wanted to do this so badly. But I was afraid that Vinnie would chase me and hurt me. I suffered through the meal, had a great night with Joyce and Kara and miserably went back to Vinnie's house to have sex and sleep.

At the end of my sophomore year at college I waved goodbye to my roommates and told them I was going home to break up with Vinnie. I know they doubted my word as I had claimed this many times. But this day there was no turning back. I drove the hour ride back to Stoughton, eager to see this play out. I stopped at home first and saw my mom hanging out by our pool. I told her I was going to dump him and she seemed surprised. I sensed she didn't want me to do this. I guess she didn't know the extent of my unhappiness. I jumped in my car and drove to his house. Vinnie had injured his leg playing softball and was on crutches. This provided me a feeling of safety as I knew he would not be able to chase after me. I walked in the door and told him this relationship had to end. I remember him chasing me with his crutches but I safely made it out to my car and back home to the pool with mom. I had no regrets and was so happy to be free.

Vinnie showed up at my house several times trying to persuade me to go back out with him. I was strong and no longer afraid. I just closed the door on him and watched him walk out of my life forever.

This was the hardest summer of my life. After two long years of putting up with crap from Vinnie I had distanced myself from all of my friends back home. My college roommates were the best but all lived at least an hour away. Joyce and Kara completely dumped me by this time and were renting a room in some beaten-down motel on Cape Cod. I really had no desire to be with them, but still felt hurt that they didn't even ask me to visit them. I had no way of meeting anyone as I had no one to even go to a bar or party with. But I did have one thing - a friend with benefits. I will get to this story after we further explore the lessons learned from Vinnie.

So if you think you are ready to get out, how do you even begin to build yourself back up?

While still in a relationship with Vinnie I decided to secretly go see a therapist. I can't imagine where I even got the idea but thank god I did. He was a brilliant man and in our one and only session he asked me what things made me happy. I was speechless and couldn't think of anything outside of Vinnie, even though it was Vinnie that was making me miserable. I tried to convince the therapist that there was a lot of good in Vinnie. He gently cut me off and asked what made me happy outside of Vinnie. I thought for a few silent moments and began talking about arts and crafts. He asked me when the last time I enjoyed this hobby was. I hadn't been to the craft store in two years, not since Vinnie and I started dating. He asked me why and we both knew it was because I was in a sick and controlling relationship.

I left his office and went straight to the craft store. I bought a bunch of Styrofoam balls, pipe cleaners and plastic eyes and went home to do my first project in years. I made a pile of animals and funny creatures out of my crafts and lost track of time. My mom was in the hospital at this point for a back injury and my dad and I went to visit her that evening with all of my Styrofoam creatures. She loved each and every one of them.

I continued to do my crafts and spend longer and longer intervals away from Vinnie. He knew something was up when I stayed at college the last two weekends of the semester. I just stopped caring and knew I was making my plan to leave, which I did shortly after that memorable therapy session. I never looked back and was so happy to be rid of this man forever.

So the therapist helps but how do you actually walk away?

The first thing you need to do is start changing your mindset. Instead of believing that the relationship will get better you need to start believing that you will get out. Give up on trying to fix it at this point and get ready to fix yourself. It can take some longer than others to make the break - but when you are ready, you *will* get out.

Remember all of the friends you had prior to meeting this guy? Many times abusive men do everything in their power to sabotage all of your healthy relationships. They will be rude to your friends, make you feel guilty for going out with them and even refrain from delivering your telephone messages to you. This gives them more control over you.

You might continue to feel isolated and dependent on this abusive guy because he just might be all that you have left. Go find those friends and tell them you are ready to leave. You will be surprised how quickly some of them will come around and help you. They left because they didn't like watching how he treated you or they just didn't like him. Now that you are ready to walk away from him they will be happy for you. Building your support system back up is going to contribute to your strength and you will be able to see the breakup through. I was unfortunate and had very few friends near me at this point in my life. I was strong and determined so I survived, but with the help of friends it would have been that much easier.

If you are in imminent danger reach out to one of the many domestic violence centers in your community. They are far more qualified to handle a dangerous situation than anyone. Trust that they are skilled in keeping you safe, protecting your confidentiality and getting you through one of the most difficult times in your life.

So, in a nutshell, what exactly should I be doing?

Abusive men are sick and need help. And you cannot be the one to help or fix the abuser. I became co-dependent in this relationship and sacrificed all of my own needs to try and fix or protect a man that I was growing to hate.

If you are being abused by someone please nurture yourself back to a better place. Your partner is never going to do this for you because they like you weak and insecure. When you are in a relationship with an abusive person, he will do whatever it takes to make you feel badly about yourself. It is time for you to take control of your life and get the help you need. Remind yourself that you deserve better than this.

9 - SCOTT

At the end of my sophomore year at SMU I spent a great deal of time hanging out with my college roommate Mary, who is still one of my closest friends today. Mary and Keith were a couple, and everyone loved them. They were a blast to hang out with! We drank, smoked pot from time to time and had many great experiences together. Keith always had a few nice roommates hanging around with him and one was named Scott.

Scott was sort of convenient for me to spend time with. I wasn't super attracted to him but I thought he was cute, sweet and easy to be around. He was a good looking guy and always had a friendly smile on his face. Scott had blue eyes, thin, light brown hair and was just a bit taller than me with a pretty good build. I never felt huge sparks but wasn't grossed out either, and I needed someone to take my mind off of Vinnie. Scott was always ready and willing. So when Keith and Mary would drift off to the bedroom, Scott and I would be left hanging out together. For a while we would just laugh, talk and stuff ourselves with some late night munchies while enjoying our good buzz.

One night after a few too many drinks, Scott invited me up to his bedroom and we fooled around for the first time. It was more comical than anything else. I remember Scott being funny and taking my bra off and then hanging it from the ceiling fan. We were just being silly and pretending the night got even wilder than it really did. In fact, my bra coming off was as far as it went back then.

The semester quickly came to an end and Scott and I exchanged phone numbers. After the official dumping of Vinnie was final I needed to have a little fun! Forget about all of my unavailable friends, I was going to spend some time with my soon-to-be "friend with benefits." I called Scott and he invited me to come to a party with his friends. I was so relieved to get out of Stoughton and take my mind off of Vinnie, as well as Joyce and Kara.

Scott knew how to show me a good time. He took me to a party on the beach with a bunch of cute guys. Scott was cool about it and just introduced me as "Jaimy" as opposed to his "date." I liked that because I was really interested in flirting and just having some fun. We drank Jell-O shots, played football on the beach and later a bunch of us sat around telling jokes, talking about sex and sharing funny, personal stories. Scott never touched me during the entire party and I was even lucky enough to exchange phone numbers with the brother of one of Scott's friends. Scott and I had an understanding, and this was working out quite well for both of us.

It got late, and Scott drove us back to his house. His mom gave me permission to sleep in the basement on the futon as it was about a 45-minute ride back home. Scott kissed me goodnight on the cheek and went upstairs to his bed. I was actually fine with this as my mind was on the cute guy that took my number. But, like I said, Scott and I had an understanding and I wanted to live up to my end of the agreement. He snuck back into the basement after his mother was safely asleep. He crawled under the blanket next to me and we took our clothes off and "fooled around." At that time, fooling around was a term used to describe some heavy foreplay without actually having sex. Remember, I was always afraid of those STDs and unplanned pregnancies, so I avoided sex at all costs.

Scott and I continued this for the entire summer and into the beginning of our junior year at SMU. There were no fireworks going off but the chemistry was just fine. I was more interested in his companionship and attention than fooling around, but it was all worth it. We were classic friends with benefits. Actually, I needed the friendship and Scott needed the benefits. The arrangement worked out well for a while and amicably faded away when we both started dating other people.

So are there any rules for having a friend with benefits?

Be sure that you both have a clear understanding of the arrangement. This can easily fail when one person in the relationship is always hoping and expecting more. Be honest with yourself. Is this really an effort to try and entice him into falling in love with you? Women typically have a bigger emotional connection to a sexual partner than men do and are usually the first to be let down in a friends with benefits relationship. Be sure to define the relationship and set the ground rules up front. Can you go to social functions together, how will you handle holidays and birthdays, do you cuddle after sex? And lastly you need to have a break-up plan in place. If one of you starts dating someone else you need to clarify how it will be communicated and be sure it is done immediately so no one ends up waiting around or being more hurt than necessary.

Are there any downfalls to this arrangement?

Friends with benefits does have its downfalls. Most will convince themselves that they are just passing time with this person until something better comes along. But you are really missing out on many opportunities to meet that right person and are settling for a relationship that lacks so many of the perks of *actually* being in a real romantic relationship. Sure, you have someone to have sex with, but it doesn't include the feelings of falling in love, holding hands, sharing your day-to-day activities together, and feeling special. You are sacrificing a great deal to have the benefit of sex with another person which I think is a pretty weak benefit. Essentially what I hear this guy saying is, "you are good enough to have sex with, but not good enough to fall in love with." However if there is a clear agreement in place, than it can work for a limited time.

So, in a nutshell, what exactly should I be doing?

Having someone to have sex with on a regular basis can be a great thing. But having casual sex with a friend that doesn't love and adore you is going to get old pretty quickly. If you are doing this to pass some time or get you through a tough break-up, then by all means go for it and make the most of it! We are all adults, sex feels good and as long as it is safe and the arrangement is clear then no harm done.

But when you are with someone that you are falling in love with, the sex will likely keep getting better and better.

Your inhibitions will be lowered and you will feel safe and comfortable to share your innermost fantasies and thoughts. When you are in a close, committed relationship you are free to explore all of this. When you are having a casual sexual relationship with a friend it simply could become routine sex, might often require alcohol and can leave you feeling lonely when the deed is done. Just don't waste too much time with this guy so you don't miss an opportunity to find that person that you are truly meant to be with.

10 - SULLY

Sully was the typical Irish, party guy. He was cute and I loved how tall he stood. He had this pasty complexion with brownish/reddish thick hair, big, round blue eyes and a beer in his hand almost every time we were together. He and I met outside an Irish pub while attending SMU and began dating in my junior year.

Sully was one of the funniest people I ever met in my life. We laughed a lot and I loved how goofy and silly he was. Sully was the guy that could put a smile on my face without even saying a single word. One of the funniest memories occurred the morning after he and a couple of his roommates spent the night at our house. Sully woke up early, climbed out of my bed and whispered to me that he was going to get up and make us all a special breakfast. I thought that was so cool, especially considering that our kitchen was stocked with very little food. Regardless, I heard pots and pans banging away, and could only imagine what this guy would create. When he yelled "breakfast is ready," our roommates dragged themselves out of bed and ran to the kitchen, only to find eight paper plates set out with a stale donut on each one. My roommate Chrissy always brought donuts back from her weekends home as her dad drove a Hostess truck. It seemed the only food we ever had was an abundance of donuts and cupcakes. We laughed and enjoyed our stale donuts. Back in college we would eat just about anything!

Sully made me laugh for about half of my junior year at college. He would stay the night and we would spend long, lazy Saturday afternoons lying on the couch, laughing and talking for hours. I genuinely liked his company. This was the first real guy that I actually had conversations with and got to know a little bit. I was shy around other guys and feared that if I said too much they wouldn't like me. It was a huge insecurity that seemed to disappear when I was with Sully.

Right before I began dating Sully I had a brief relationship with one of his roommates. His name was Brian and he had a way of bringing out all of my insecurities. To start with, he was short and I was so self-conscious about being tall. He was one of the many guys that left me feeling shy and awkward and never really got to know me. Clearly this was a turn off and he dumped me after about three short weeks. In the end it worked out well because I got the chance to start dating Sully who never made me feel insecure or self-conscious. We went fun places like the dog track, parties and even hit a restaurant from time to time. We would always laugh at the silliest things and seemed to share an unusual sense of humor. I looked forward to being with him, enjoyed having sex with him and liked his companionship. But one day I decided to end it.

We went to Boston on New Year's Eve with Chrissy and Albie, our roommates who were also in a relationship. Albie was a complete dick to me and could ruin just about any time. He would make fun of the way I looked, my nose, my walk and anything I said. I still to this day have no idea why he targeted me. It wasn't funny, flirty or cute! It basically made me miserable. Sully never wanted conflict with anyone and just tried to laugh the whole thing off in an effort to keep the peace.

Well, that New Year's Eve sucked, to be honest. It was freezing and we just went from cab to cab with no real plan. Albie was especially witty with his Jaimy jokes that evening. I was annoyed with the whole scene and wanted to be warm and in a cozy bed. The four of us tried to share a king-sized bed in our cheap hotel room and I rolled on the floor in annoyance. Sully rolled down next to me and I broke up with him right there and then. For whatever reason, I just didn't want to have sex with him or do much of anything. I know that Sully never teamed up with Albie and never participated in any of Albie's teasing. In fact, he was the nicest guy I had ever dated. But nice wasn't working for me that night. I would have been more pleased by a bully that smashed Albie in the face.

Sully may have had no idea that the situation with Albie was actually upsetting me as much as it did. I never told him how I felt and would just get into little debates with Albie and hoped Sully would help me put a stop to this behavior. He never did. He rolled on that floor next to me and whispered some sweet compliments hoping our relationship would resume as always. But it never did.

Why is it that so many women don't just share their feelings?

Many women love to complain that their husbands or boyfriends do things that annoy or upset them. And quite frankly, many husbands can be quite annoying and inconsiderate. Some would claim that their spouses continually downplay birthdays and anniversaries. Other times they are angry that their spouses or boyfriends don't help out more with the kids, chores or errands. And the most common complaint that I hear is that these men are not around enough. Sometimes they work long hours and other times they just hide out in their man cave.

Many of these ladies never come right out and say what they feel and need. Typically, they spend tons of energy convincing themselves that no matter how much they complain nothing will ever change. And to some extent, this may be true. But it will not always be true! So instead, they take on a passive-aggressive attitude and go through the motions of being married while constantly complaining about it.

Some women like to have drama in their lives because that is familiar to them and they aren't even aware this pattern is happening. These women often have friends in a similar situation and get pleasure out of engaging in these venting sessions. Others don't believe their needs are valuable or important so they just continually suppress them until they just can't stand it anymore and the relationship blows up.

I remember years ago when a close friend of mine was so annoyed because her husband went to the grocery store and came home with some frozen dinners. I was thinking, wow, a guy that actually goes grocery shopping - but she was thinking something else. My friend was so angry at her husband because he didn't know her well enough to know that she would never eat frozen dinners.

Sure, he was at fault for not paying close enough attention to the habits of his wife. But we know that most men are guilty of this. If they make a mistake, give them the benefit of the doubt and just tell them what your needs are. In most cases, they are not intending to annoy or neglect you. In fact, in this situation I think he thought he was saving her the trouble of cooking so many meals each week. He was simply wrong and made a mistake. If he goes back to the grocery store the following week and still fails to buy you the type of food you like, then you will have a case for being really annoyed.

So, if we are feeling that our needs are not going to be met, what should we do?

First, identify the things that you want and the things that really matter to you. Now don't be unrealistic and expect your hard-working, middle-class lifestyle to drastically change overnight. But think about the small things that will meet your needs. Would it help if he cooked dinner one night a week, or dropped the kids off at school on certain days? Once you identify what exactly it is that he can do to make you happier then you need to set up a good time to talk to him about it. Just be sure it isn't during PMS or in the heat of a fight as this might set you up to completely fail.

If your birthday is coming up, don't waste energy telling your friends that you just know he is going to ignore the day again. Tell him ahead of time that you would like to do something special for your birthday. I understand that there are a few rare men out there that instinctively do these romantic things for their wives, but your spouse may not be one of them. And I have to say that I know very few men who are so thoughtful. If you are looking for reasons to end the relationship and want something to be unhappy about, then by all means, continue the pattern of not expressing what you really want.

So, in a nutshell, what should I be doing?

If you want to have a happy relationship, then share your needs and accept the relationship for what it is. I am in a relationship today where birthdays and anniversaries are very unimportant. This would infuriate many of my friends. But I am elated by the attention I get *every day* from this man. I have other friends who get an overdose of flowers and jewelry on Valentine's Day, and are so proud of how thoughtful their husbands are. Of course they are the ones complaining that their husbands work too much or are emotionally unavailable.

Every relationship that is worth having must possess some positive traits. Be thankful for the wonderful things you have. If there is something more you want, then ask for it. If he can't provide you with this, then you can either accept the relationship for what it is and be happy with it or move on. Just don't ever sit around and complain day after day without ever clearly telling him exactly what it is that you need.

I can't leave this chapter without asking you to accept the fact that we all have different personality traits, and you can't expect miracles. But before you complain or throw in the towel on the relationship, just be sure you have clearly expressed what exactly it is that will make you happy.

11- JEROME

For anyone that has ever worked in a restaurant, you must know what happens between the waitresses and the cooks. We all work long exhausting shifts and don't see too many other people outside of the restaurant. Typically after our shift we tend to travel in packs to a local bar with a late last call or just grab a drink right at our place of work. Horizons was a beautiful restaurant and a great place to waitress. It sat on the beach in Sandwich, MA, the tips were huge and my co-workers were a blast. It was also the perfect place to hang out after work, as we often did.

His name was Jerome and he was only 5'7" with dark tight curls and a mustache. He had a big face with big features - his nose, lips and eyes were all just a bit exaggerated in size. He was the first Greek I ever had a crush on. Although I am not sure this was actually my crush, I think Jerome was the one with the crush in this story.

Jerome was very popular among the waitresses, but wasn't really my type. It was mostly the height thing that got to me. I was close to 5'9" with long legs that made me appear even taller. Almost every time I saw Jerome I was wearing my waitressing uniform which consisted of a tan mini skirt, a tight blue t-shirt with the Horizons logo across the chest, white socks and sneakers. I looked great in a mini skirt and Jerome was never afraid to say it. Looking back, his comments bordered on sexual harassment, but I loved the attention and wasn't going to complain to anyone about it. We are all guilty of liking a good ego boost once in a while, even if we are not all that interested in the guy giving it to us, right?

Jerome was my favorite cook and if he was on shift I knew it was going to be a fun night. He knew that fried clams were my favorite and whenever I arrived to work he would have a plate of them waiting for me under the heat lamps. He had a massive crush on me, and even though many waitresses fought for his attention I was the one that got it all. He complimented me every time I entered the kitchen to collect my dinners, he often asked me out, made passes at me and tried every trick in the book to get me back to his house.

There was a crowd of us that began hanging out together and we all had Mondays off. We turned Mondays into what we called our "field trip" days. Most of these Mondays we would hang out at my parents beach, which was a favorite spot for everyone. It was a private beach open to a group of homes in my parent's neighborhood. Jerome had no complaints because he got to check me out in my bikini, which I was very proud to wear.

My mom was big on taking pictures and was also big on me finding a boyfriend. She pushed Jerome and me together any chance she had. On one particular day, she requested we pose for a picture together. I was in the ocean standing by a huge rock. Jerome was funny and climbed up on the rock and put his arm around me to pose for the picture. That was the one and only moment that he was taller than me.

The summer was a blast. Jerome, Dave, Neil, Stacey and a few others worked the same shifts as I did, and we partied together after work and hung out on our days off. I loved sitting in the hot sun with my feet in the sand, smelling the ocean water. There were always friends coming to visit us as we were the lucky ones with the beautiful house on the most desirable beach on Cape Cod. By nighttime, I was ready for a fast-paced shift at Horizons where I could flirt with Jerome and go out drinking with my crowd of friends after work. It was the ideal situation for a college student and it was the best summer of my life.

One night towards the end of the summer, Jerome and I were enjoying a few beers on the patio of Horizons after our shift. Our friends were with us and all acting as Jerome's wingmen. They were pushing the two of us together, and Jerome and I pretended we were going to hook up. I even sat on his lap after Neil offered to pay for the tab if I complied. Everyone seemed to be invested in Jerome and me hooking up. Everyone but me, actually, but I was drunk and feeling great so I thought, *why not?*

The night was ending, and Jerome looked at me with those huge puppy dog eyes and invited me back to his house. I shocked him and said yes. We went back to Jerome's house and to avoid his roommates we hung out in Jerome's room. It got pretty heated and we found ourselves lying in our underwear kissing on his bed. It was fun but I wasn't having sex with this guy because I still liked that I could count my sexual partners on one hand. Besides, I knew this would never lead to anything romantic and I didn't want to have any regrets. At one point I asked Jerome if it was shocking to have me lying almost naked in his bed. He said it was exactly how he had pictured it a million times in his head.

I tried hard to be into this guy, but the truth was I just didn't feel any chemistry. I was actually feeling the chemistry with someone else who wasn't exactly available. I will share this story in the next chapter. Chemistry is a real thing and without it you will never be happy. In psychology, the word "chemistry" is used when describing a connection between two people. When two people have "chemistry," they feel a natural attraction to each other with no effort whatsoever.

I have heard many stories about women who were dating perfect men. These guys called when they said they would, showed great respect and treated them like princesses. Yet they were battling the big chemistry question in their heads constantly. These are some of the typical questions I would get.

How could I break up with someone that treats me so well when this was all I ever wanted?

Really, is that all you ever wanted? Having a guy treat you well is only half of the battle. You need to find someone that treats you well who you are physically attracted to. My sister married a great guy about 15 years ago. I am a big fan of my brother-in-law. He has an awesome body, some sexy tattoos and he is a nice down-to-earth guy. My sister looks great too, but back when they were married she became practical and matronly looking. One day we met in Boston with the kids and she was wearing a practical and warm blue winter coat. I showed up in a leather jacket with a trendy wool hat. She made a crack about why I would wear a leather coat in the winter. I responded by telling her she was far too matronly looking to understand. Stacey said that was the biggest insult I ever gave her.

Stacey and Edward got along great. They were like best friends. They enjoyed working out together, had two beautiful kids and a nice home on Cape Cod. But Stacey and Edward had no chemistry. They both knew it and convinced themselves that most couples didn't have sex. They divorced and a few years later Edward found a beautiful girl with which the physical attraction was powerful. My sister is still single and dating but she threw out that blue jacket and invested in a wardrobe that made her feel sexy again. She too began dating and was reminded of what it would feel like to have that instant sexual chemistry again.

Is there something wrong with me? This guy seems perfect!

Yes, it is true you met a "perfect" guy this time. But the reality is that he is perfect for your best friend, co-worker or maybe your sister. Just because he is nice doesn't mean you should sacrifice chemistry. And just because you have a mutual instant chemistry doesn't mean you should sacrifice being treated well. In order to have a successful long-lasting relationship you need to have both chemistry and respect.

There are so many deal breakers that singles hold onto. Some women require a certain educational level, want a mutual religious belief and need specific physical criteria. As women get older they become less and less concerned with their deal breaker lists. There are only two major deal breakers that need to stay on that list, and they are respect and physical attraction. Once you find both of these it is possible to get past some of those other deal breakers.

Doesn't chemistry eventually fade in every relationship?

No! Chemistry does not fade in every relationship and this is one of those lies that irritate me to no end! I hear stories about many unhealthy and unhappy relationships all of the time. I find it very sad that so many people stay in such miserable situations. But even sadder is when these people preach and try to convince their single friends that this is inevitable. If you are going to be miserable, could you please keep it to yourself?

When I met my husband, the chemistry was instant. I was so attracted to him and loved our sexual relationship. I had those miserable friends and they always claimed it would die out in a couple of years. After three years passed and I got pregnant with our son Trevor, they all claimed having another child would kill our sex life. Now after 10 years together, our sexual relationship is still as strong as when we met. Sure, there are many nights when sleep becomes the priority and waking up in the middle of the night to have sex is totally not in the plan. But what I am saying is that I still enjoy kissing him, love when we do find time alone and am never repulsed when he touches me.

So, in a nutshell, what do I need to know?

You *can* have it all, and it all starts with believing it is available to you. The two things you can never sacrifice are chemistry and respect. But your relationship must have both of these traits at the same time. When you have chemistry without respect you will be treated poorly. I have heard many women say that the sex is great and they are afraid to give it up. I can assure those women that if he keeps mistreating you, then the sex won't be great forever.

And then there are those women who are treated so well by their boyfriends but the chemistry is non-existent. These women will likely get bored and constantly wonder what else is out there. But when you have both chemistry and respect you can fall into a very happy and successful long-term relationship. And please, when those miserable friends try to convince you that this is totally unrealistic, just come back and reread this chapter.

12 - JACK

When I picture Jack today, the image of Kenny Chesney comes to mind. Kenny Chesney is my absolute favorite celebrity in the world. And he just happens to look a lot like Jack. Jack was in the military full-time and spent some evenings bartending at a local dive called The Fish Hook. I was in college at this time and came home for summer breaks and waitressed at Horizons, which was about a mile away from The Fish Hook.

My sister Stacey, her boyfriend Paul and I often found ourselves hanging out at the Fish Hook. Beer was cheap, they had a dart board and there was always a fun crowd. I remember the first time we visited this local dive. It was after my night shift at Horizons.

Typically I was still wearing my Horizons uniform, but after a while I would keep a sexy halter top in my car and change into it after my shift. I worked out constantly in those days and had a fantastic body. My legs were naturally long and had great muscle tone. I could still pull off a size four and had curves in all the right places. Although my boobs were still small, my mom always treated me to the best bras that could do wonders for my almost B breasts. I was living with my parents who had a home on the beach, allowing me to maintain the perfect tan. I had highlights in my hair and would always wear braids and hairclips to keep it looking cute.

That first night, Jack was standing behind the bar mixing drinks for the crowd of customers. He was fit, had dark brown hair with a crew cut, blue eyes and a hot smile. He asked for our order, and we all got beers. Jack and I made eye contact and he shot me a very flirtatious smile. I felt my stomach drop and thought *I have to have this guy*. My sister, Paul and I enjoyed our beers and played some darts, all while I continued to make eye contact with this hot bartender.

A few beers later I was ready to abandon my third wheel status with Stacey and Paul and sat down at the bar. Jack and I talked in a rather intense, flirtatious way. I have no idea what we said and it really didn't matter. I got up to use the bathroom, which was right by the kitchen in the back end of the restaurant. As I stood in line waiting for the bathroom, Jack snuck up behind me, put his hand on my waist and directed me into the small kitchen that had been shut down and abandoned by this point in the evening. There was not a single word spoken. When we reached the back of the kitchen he lifted me up on the counter and began making out with me. It was by far the sexiest and hottest kiss I had experienced at that point in my life.

After the kiss he pulled away and just stared at my face. I stared back and still nothing but a smile was shared. He put his hand on my cheek and touched me rather gently as he traced my face with his hand. I just stared at him, almost hypnotized by all that was happening. I snapped out of it as I suddenly felt he had a ring on his finger. I hoped to hell it was a class ring or perhaps some military paraphernalia. I grabbed his hand and studied the wedding band on his left ring finger. I finally broke our silence and asked him if he was married. Jack replied and said "I am afraid so."

I was almost 21 years old with a fake ID, and visited the Fish Hook every chance I had. Jack and I continued to meet in the kitchen for our sexy make-out sessions about three times a week. Stacey, Paul and I would close the place down, and after last call Jack would pour himself a stiff drink and sit down at our table. Jack would touch my legs and hold my hand under the table as if no one noticed. Part of the excitement was that I knew it was wrong. Keeping it a secret just added to the thrill.

One night his shift ended early. I didn't have my car, as I had hitched a ride with Stacey and Paul. Jack asked me to take a spin on his motorcycle. There was nothing hotter than sitting on the back of this guy's motorcycle with my arms around his waist. He rode straight to a motel and asked me if I would like to spend some time with him. I jumped off the bike and eagerly followed his sexy body up to the motel room. I wondered if he had planned this. But he never knew when I was going to show up at the bar and never had any way to reach me. So it made no sense that he had secured a motel room just for the two of us.

When he opened the door, I saw so many of his belongings scattered about the motel room. Clothes were thrown across the floor, all his toiletries lied on the shelf next to the bathroom sink, and it was clear that Jack had been staying in this motel for days and maybe even weeks. I never asked any questions but it was evident that he was going through some marital problems. I am not sharing this to rationalize the relationship. I am just trying to paint a clear picture. Jack and I had many motorcycle rides, late night walks on the beach and overnights in that motel room. He never said that he and his wife were separated or that he intended to leave her, he never told me he loved me, never took me on a real date, never called me and never told anyone about us. This was the quintessential affair!

I carried this relationship on for longer than I care to admit. The truth is, the only reason it ended was because I graduated from college moved away to Boston and got a job outside of my waitressing job. Every now and then I popped back home to see my parents and would stop into The Fish Hook. Jack was always happy to see me and I loved to see him light up when I walked in. But eventually the day came that I never saw him again. Who knows what happened to this guy. It has been 20 years and for all I know he is still pouring drinks at The Fish Hook.

Why do women have affairs with married men?

There are so many reasons why single women have affairs with married men. Some find it exciting and like the thrill of having to keep it a secret. Others don't even know the man is married until they are deeply invested in the relationship. But for me, I never planned it. I simply saw this man and felt an uncontrollable chemistry. The bigger question is why I didn't stop it sooner. Affairs are typically exhilarating, passionate and even romantic. I had never felt such hot and intense sparks before and stupidly carried it on hoping somehow he would be mine. I got to feel all of these wonderful things with this gorgeous military officer. But at the same time I got to feel lonely, demeaned, and let down on a continuous basis.

Does someone always get hurt in this type of situation?

Jack and I were lucky because this affair just sort of faded away over time. We escaped our affair with little damage to either of us. But this is not usually the case. Most cause damage to the many people involved, including children. Jack had two children. As far as I know, he and his wife were having marital problems before we met and I don't think she ever knew about us, but I really don't know for sure. I like to think that the affair was a result of the unhappy marriage as opposed to the unhappy marriage being a result of the affair.

I know so many married people that are in unhappy relationships. Some of them have affairs while others don't even see it as an option. Some leave before the marriage takes them to the world of infidelity while others need the affair to give them the motivation to end the marriage. Most end up hurt, feeling guilty and regretting all of it.

So you have such great memories of this man, do you think that there are times when having an affair is acceptable?

In a perfect world, I would discourage anyone from living through this drama. But I have some close girlfriends who are in marriages that leave them emotionally and/or physically lonely. They claim to love their husbands and have no desire to tear apart their families. But some of them have confessed to me that they are having affairs and most with little regret. I almost think in some of these cases their husbands know and choose to turn the other cheek to keep the peace in these relationships. I am not supporting having this type of affair, I am just saying that I understand the pain they are in and I understand how and why they find this fulfilling. But the one question that I always ask them is how they see their affairs ending. Either they will get caught or not. The risk is huge and I know many that could never cope with the fear and guilt associated with getting caught. I, for one, fall into that category. But I am not passing judgment on these friends. As I always say, just be careful.

I was a single women looking to be loved and adored by a man. I wanted someone to make me feel special and someday wanted to be married with a family. I could have wasted endless years with this man. In some sense having great, passionate sex whenever I wanted with a man I desired may not sound like wasting time. But what was happening was that during this time I was unavailable to meet someone that would fall truly in love with me. Whenever I did meet guys, I compared them to this fairytale affair I was having. The truth is that I barely knew this man that I claimed to adore. We didn't talk a whole lot and the entire relationship was based on physical chemistry.

True love is when you know someone inside and outside of the bedroom. You need to experience one's bad habits, appreciate their passions and understand the true core of their existence. My affair wasn't even close to this. I deserved to find a man that was physically available to join me in life. I deserved someone that I could proudly bring around my family and dance with at my friends' weddings.

So, in a nutshell, what should I do?

Don't convince yourself that you are just passing time with this guy and enjoying the ride until something better comes along. I can assure you that you are missing many opportunities to meet Mr. Right if you are spending most of your time with Mr. Married. If you are not experiencing all the wonderful perks of being in a relationship, then you need to keep looking. If this man ever intends to leave his wife for you then the risk of losing you is what will push him into action. But I am sorry to say that in most cases, the men are enticed by the sex and will let you walk away before breaking up his family. He likely won't initiate ending the affair, and you have to be the brave one to end it. Free yourself up to find a relationship that offers you everything you deserve.

13 - STEVEN

Steven was yet another tall, dark and handsome guy. I was just out of college and got my first job as a Behavior Therapist at a residential treatment center for autistic adults in Boston, Massachusetts. Behavior Therapist was just a fancy name for a direct care worker. Steven was one of the supervisors and he happened to be the best Behavior Therapist in the house. He had this funky hairstyle that was long in the front and cut short around the back. His eyes were dark, intense and mysterious. Steven was a big guy and I always liked that. He was the type that would always make you feel protected. Steven was the best-looking guy at work and many of the other girls were interested and intrigued by him. This made him even more appealing to me, and I was determined to steal his attention.

My first intense encounter with Steve was when one of the highly aggressive autistic clients had a violent episode and attacked me. I was on the ground in a double fisted hair pull, my arm locked in his clenched teeth while I yelled for assistance. Steven was the first one to come to my rescue and always the one you would want to see at a time like this. He easily intervened and freed me from this volatile person. I was then escorted out of the building and to the local hospital for neck and back injuries. I turned the corner on my way out and saw Steven watching me walk away. I simply melted. For a moment I forgot about my injuries and felt a surge of excitement that Steven had finally acknowledged my existence.

We dated for a while after this incident, and moved in together sooner than we should have. I had my own apartment but my roommate and best friend, Pauline, got a better job offer and was moving away. I could have gotten another roommate but it seemed more fun to play house with my new boyfriend. We combined our two households and shared an apartment in Boston, Massachusetts.

He was passionate about the arts and music. Most of the bands he liked were unheard of to me. But I tried to get into his music and actually grew to like some of it. We were quite different, as he had many interests and hobbies and I basically just wanted to find a boyfriend. Steven loved to cook and I was happy to eat anything he made. Steven liked theater, baseball and museums and I went along to share in his passions. After a year we were both a little bored and thought it would be fun to move away. We quit our jobs, sold our furniture packed up the cats and drove south. We landed in a great apartment in Baltimore, Maryland overlooking Camden Yards. Steven was a big baseball fan and he was happy to cheer on the Orioles from our rooftop deck.

He and I spent four years in Baltimore, and they were pretty intense years. After about two years of living there, I arrived home from work one day, surprised to find a path of candles, my favorite Harry Connick, Jr. CD playing and a homemade dinner on the kitchen table. And the biggest surprise of all was Steven holding that little square box that

I waited so long for. He proposed and the wedding plans began. I was thrilled to pick out my sexy wedding gown, travel back home to find a venue, disc jockey, flowers and all of the details that go into planning that special day.

About nine months before our big day, Steven and I drove back to Plymouth, Massachusetts to see our families and celebrate our engagement. I stayed at my parents' house while Steven was about 15 minutes away with his family. The next morning, I was awoken to my dad screaming that my mother had been in a car accident. Dad and I ran to the scene of the crime, which was at the top of my parents' street. There was my mother, lying on a stretcher with a bloody sheet over her face.

We buried my mom that weekend - and my life changed forever. Just a month prior, Mom and Dad visited us in Baltimore. We shopped for my wedding gown and we both knew the minute I put the third one on that it was perfect. I had no idea that would be the last time we shopped together or that she wouldn't be there at Plimouth Plantation on June 15 to see me marry Steven. Steven worked hard to make the whole planning process fun. He knew the enormous pain I was coping with and was incredibly strong through my grieving. His mother helped me pick out flowers, my dad took my dress in for alterations and friends and family pulled together to make the day beautiful. June 15, 1996 was a bright and sunny day. Seconds before I walked down the aisle my dad approached me with a final hug and kiss. I looked and saw a lady bug on his suit jacket. Ladybugs were my mom's favorite thing. The tears started as the music began to play. I walked down the aisle knowing in my heart that she was with me. Steven and I shared in our marriage vows and had the most beautiful reception. It was a fairy tale wedding!

In many ways we loved each other. He was a funny guy who made me laugh and was a true friend to me for many years. Steven helped me to get through the loss of my mom and was very supportive to me during such a difficult time.

Eventually we decided it would be best to move back north and start a family. We landed jobs in the Hartford, Connecticut area and made West Hartford our permanent home. In 1999, I gave birth to our beautiful son, Matthew.

Steven and I both adored this child to no end. He stayed up endless hours rocking and singing to his son. We both lit up every time Matthew was nearby and neither of us ever in a million years wanted to be removed from seeing him on a daily basis. Nor did we ever want to cause him a minute of pain. But the reality was that Steven and I were not in love anymore. We continued to go through the motions of being married and raising a child together. But we both knew that the passion, love and romance had simply died. We tried therapy and worked hard to salvage our relationship.

Steven was the brave one. I would have stayed a long time, perhaps forever, because I had so many fears. I was afraid to leave. I was afraid to be alone. I feared no one else would ever fall in love with me and I feared how this would affect our son. Steve proceeded with the separation and although at the time I dreaded what was happening I had no choice. We filed for a very amicable divorce, didn't pay a dime for attorneys and worked out the visitation arrangements with no help from anyone. It was a quick and easy process and we were able to move forward with our lives and adjusted to our new family status.

Do you believe that it is right to stay together for the sake of the children?

I have read studies that said children of divorced families suffered far more than those whose parents stayed together. Did any of these studies compare the effects on a child when parents stayed in a loveless or unhappy marriage?

Staying together for sake of the children is quite possibly an excuse for being too afraid to walk away. I know this for sure as I was once convincing myself of this. I remember a friend telling me they were getting divorced and I was actually jealous because I knew that someday I would be there but didn't have the strength to get there yet. Steven was always smart and a realist. He knew that this marriage had to end and to this day I am thankful that he initiated the process.

Steven and I have both remarried into happy, healthy relationships. Matthew now has role models of what loving couples are supposed to look like. He is able to see how two people that love each other should behave. If you have convinced yourself that you are doing what is best for your children, I believe you are quite simply wrong. I won't deny that it is traumatic and that the older the children get the harder it can be. But what I am saying is that when a parent is in an unhappy or unhealthy relationship, they are teaching their children to sacrifice their own happiness. Therefore I am saying that, in my opinion, it is not best to stay in a miserable situation just for the children.

But what do you do when you are just so afraid to leave? Besides wait for him to do it, as you did?

If you are unhappy in the relationship it is likely that your partner is too. Many times women are afraid to hurt their spouse. Especially in situations where there is no abuse, no fighting and nothing overtly wrong. But when two people have fallen out of love and therapy has failed to rescue the relationship, it is time to begin talking with your spouse about next steps. Many women that feared bringing up this subject were pleasantly surprised by their husband's willingness to proceed with the divorce. Others had to take a different approach.

My sister in law, Heather, stayed in one of these relationships for years. We all knew that she was preparing to leave and it took her well over a year to facilitate the process. One morning her husband left for work and an entire crew of people that adored Heather came to her rescue. Family and friends arrived at Heather's house just minutes after her husband drove off to work. They packed up all her belongings, loaded their cars and moved Heather to her beautiful new apartment. Perhaps it wasn't beautiful, but it was all hers. She had a space to raise her children that was free of any fighting, pain and unhappiness.

We all worried about how her husband would react, and the truth is he saw it coming the whole time. He did not freak out, act violently or even try to woo her back. This exit was a lot easier than anyone anticipated. I am not suggesting this is the best way to do it. But if having an amicable conversation about a separation fails then this may be an option.

Others rely solely on the legal system. They hire an attorney, have their husband served divorce papers and leave all of the communication up to lawyers who make a small fortune. This is the more expensive way to go, but if the relationship is full of hostility, the spouse is mentally ill or just completely unreasonable then this may be the best option.

So, in a nutshell, what do I need to do?

If this chapter feels very reminiscent of your life but you are still having trouble accepting it, I am going to tell you to be honest with yourself. Admit that it is time to start thinking about how you will get out.

The first step is to build your support network. Sometimes we lose touch with people we love as our relationships progress. But you are in a time of crisis and most of those friends will step up to the plate in a time of need. Accept that you are no longer in a place where you are trying to fix your relationship. And come to the realization that you are getting ready to move on. Of course you should have exhausted therapy and any other interventions to save the marriage before reaching this point.

Lastly, experience the feelings of guilt, fear and sadness. That is how you are supposed to feel when entering into a divorce that will hurt your entire family. But trust that the alternative is staying in a relationship that is making you so unhappy. You deserve better and so does your spouse. People survive divorce every day and if you are that unhappy, you will survive this too.

I understand it can be very hard to leave. One can feel paralyzed at the mere thought of ending such a long-term relationship, one in which you built a home and a family. But at the end of the day you will both be free to find love and happiness, and that is the best gift you can give your children. I know many women who have been through this and not a single one ever looked back with regret. In fact, these women all looked back and asked why they didn't do it sooner.

\

14 - JAIMY

OK, I know what you are all thinking - *Oh no, not more crap about needing to love yourself.* I remember after my divorce I was so aggravated by those who suggested self-help books to me. I didn't want to read anything, I just wanted some quick advice on how to find a guy and live happily ever after. In fact, I was quite sure that once I found the guy I would love everything, including myself.

But I realized that it took a lot more work than that. Sure, some people just get lucky and find the guy with no effort and some of us have to work a little harder at it. If you don't want to hear the part about falling in love with yourself then I have no problem if you skip to the next chapter. But I think you will be missing the most important message in this book.

In many ways I hated myself. I understand why my ex-husband didn't want to be with me - I didn't even want to be around myself. I had issues with myself both inside and out. I am going to start with my exterior.

I remember taking a photograph on Santa's lap with Matthew. I looked at the photograph and actually considered asking for a retake. It was my hair and my nose. And the winter coat I was wearing didn't help the cause. I don't have that picture anymore because I hated how I looked.

A short time later I was in that same shopping mall and I passed by a mirror. At this point I was about one month into my separation from my ex-husband. I was pushing Matthew around in his stroller, cursing in my head at every married couple I saw. The worst were the ones where the guys were pushing the strollers while the moms carried bags from Nordstrom. If you were wearing a wedding band that was another reason I would hate you. I had a scowl on my face as I convinced myself no one would ever push Matthew's stroller again but me. I caught a glimpse of myself in the mirror and hated what I saw. My hair, my nose and my angry scowl had to go.

I am not advocating that everyone have surgery but if something really upsets you and surgery is a reasonable option then I just ask you to consider it. My nose broke multiple times when I was a child. It was never fixed properly. My nose was crooked my entire life. I was made fun of through middle and high school by my peers and my sister. I never really thought of it as an option before this point. Soon after this day I called a plastic surgeon and had a free consultation. He took a picture of me, told me the price and rescheduled a follow-up visit for one week later.

I arrived that following week still not sure what to do. I was afraid of surgery and it was so expensive that I couldn't decide. A nurse walked me into the doctor's office and while I waited for him to enter I saw a picture of myself on his computer screen. I looked at the picture and decided that I really didn't look bad at all. It was actually the best picture I had ever seen of myself. I wanted to just ask the doctor to print me the photo, and I would scan it and use it as my match.com profile picture. I had made a final decision that I liked what I looked like and that the $4000 check that I was about to write was going to stay in my bank book.

When the doctor entered the room and gestured toward the picture of me on the screen, he asked, "what do you think?" I confidently responded by telling him that I loved what I looked liked and was so sorry to have wasted so much of his time. The doctor responded by telling me that he Photoshopped the picture to create an image of what my new nose would look like after the surgery. Out came my checkbook and the surgery was scheduled.

Four thousand dollars and a painful recovery later, I decided it was worth everything. I see myself in a mirror or in a photograph today and never have to think it was ruined by my nose. I know so many people are thinking a guy should love me for me and not for my nose. But the reality is that chemistry is real. We have all met people that we were physically not attracted to for one reason or another. I know I have done it a million times. So physically looking the best you can will increase the number of people that would find you appealing.

Your outer shell is important, but we are limited to what we can do with our physical appearance. If you are pale get some sun, if you have no clue how to dress spend a little money on a style consultant and if your hair is unmanageable or out of style don't rely on Supercuts to spiff you up.

Your body should be a top priority, and luckily we have more control over this. If you are overweight, see a hypnotist and address your relationship with food, and then work with a nutritionist and a personal trainer to get your body in shape. You should do the best you can with what you have! If your nose is busted, you have moles on your face that make you self-conscious or any other imperfections that bother you, just consult with a doctor about your options.

It's important to always remember there is so much more to a person than their outer shell. Don't neglect the internal and emotional part of you. The physical shell is only half of the battle and quite frankly, I believe it is the easier half.

Now for the emotional part of what I have learned. After my divorce I spent most of my time convincing myself that I was always going to be single and that I was unlovable. I was so convincing that I actually believed these ridiculous thoughts and created situations to feed my negative thinking. I had no idea that I had any power to change this but I had to give it a shot.

I decided to first get rid of the negative beliefs. So I would write each one down on an index card and read it aloud. I would then take that card and rip it up in to a million tiny pieces. After this I would take the scraps and burn them in my fire pit. But I could still see the remains so I collected the ashes and flushed them down the toilet. I did this every night for weeks. After a few weeks of burning and flushing multiple index cards I still had a little bit of the negativity stuck in my brain. I looked at myself in the mirror and told myself that I was nuts for still having doubts about myself. I continued to talk to myself in the mirror, repeating over and over how lovable I was. The best part was, I started to believe it.

I began to feel good and treated myself to some new clothes and makeup. Prior to this I shopped at tag sales and clearance racks and never really believed I deserved to buy something straight off of a mannequin. In addition, my makeup consisted of whatever my sister became tired of and passed on to me. And I joined a gym. I was lucky in the sense that I was never overweight but in fact underweight. I looked awful and needed to build some muscle tone. I started to really fall in love with the new Jaimy and was readier than ever to start dating again.

I knew very little about Internet dating but match.com was exciting. I would wake up every morning and view all of the new profiles posted on the site. I would email the guys that I found appealing and hoped to hear back from them. I heard from many and was very smart about it. If they were unemployed, appeared to be immature or partied too much, I just moved on.

I now had standards. There was a time when the expression "out of my league" meant nothing to me. My league at one point would simply have been anyone with a pulse that treated me like crap. But it was a new day and I wanted to find a guy that was attractive, smart, funny and would fall head over heels in love with me.

My dating beliefs had drastically changed. When I would be getting ready for a date I would think about whether or not I'd be attracted to the guy. In the past I always worried about what my date would think of me. If someone didn't like me or didn't find me attractive now, I could handle it. I finally liked myself and was sure that I would find the right guy who would appreciate me. The search was fun and I was willing to view each dating experience as an opportunity to learn something new. I no longer feared being alone or being rejected. I knew that I wanted to find a partner in life and was willing to put forth the effort to make it happen.

There were some days when I would relapse and start to believe my negative thoughts for a moment. But I knew that going back to the mirror and repeating the affirmations

I had so much success with in the past would fix me right back up. It was about catching myself before I started to believe the negativity and having the willpower to change those beliefs fast. It shocks me when I hear friends attempt to convince me that they are always the victim, have had so many misfortunes and just accept that their lives suck. Some of them are willing to accept my advice and actually do the work to change these negative beliefs but many believe it is destiny. I had a friend tell me that some people are just destined to be miserable. She was exactly right! Anyone that wants to believe something so ridiculous is destined to be miserable.

My positive attitude and commitment to finding love led me to match.com where I had 13 great dates. Despite what you may have heard the only lie I ever experienced was the guy who told me he was 5'9". I am a bit tall and prefer to date taller guys. Let's just say Mr. five-foot-something was the shortest date I ever had. But all of my dates were nice guys and with a little screening and the right attitude you too can have a positive Internet dating experience.

You talked about surgery and reinventing yourself, what if I am happy with my imperfections?

If you are fully happy and love yourself the way you are then you shouldn't change a thing. I was self-conscious and didn't feel good about myself. It was the right decision for me. Just be sure that you are being honest with yourself and if you are truly happy then I am sure there is someone out there that will fully accept you.

You really are an advocate of online dating and match.com, can you share some internet dating tips?

The first thing you need to do is create your match.com profile. There is no need to spend a ton of money on professional pictures. But you should have three or four recent candid shots of yourself. Never use a picture with multiple people in the photo, especially if you are not the most attractive one in the shot. Be sure you look like your photo as eventually they will meet you and you want to be honest and up front. Write something quick and fun that will stand out. Avoid writing a book, stay away from bragging about accomplishments and let your true personality shine through.

Once your profile is up and ready to go reach out and contact singles that you find appealing. A quick message with a comment about something they shared in their profile is perfect. And remember my earlier quote from Babe Ruth, "every strike brings me closer to the next home run." Don't get discouraged if you get rejected. They are really only rejecting a few photos and a profile. Keep a positive attitude and you can meet many wonderful people.

Once you have lined up a date find out his full name prior to meeting him. Then go to google.com and search their name. This won't tell you everything but in most cases it will confirm that they are who they say they are, reveal if they have a criminal history and likely will prove where they are employed. Always meet in a public place and make the first date a quick one. Be sure to let a friend know who you are with and where you will be.

I am not a fan of pen-palling for more than a few emails but you should have a phone conversation with your date prior to meeting. You can really get a good feel for someone through a phone call. Lastly, trust your gut! If he seems weird or something is just off then you just don't go on a date with the guy.

So in a nutshell what should I do?

You should do whatever it takes to be happy with yourself both physically and mentally. And if you are looking for true love then I strongly encourage you to go speed dating, join an internet dating site and get out as much as possible. Don't listen to those friends that try to convince you that all guys are jerks or that only losers are on match.com. Something tells me that the friend giving such advice is simply not a happy person. If you want to find true love then start believing it will happen. And it will!

15 - BEN

The first guy I dated after my divorce was named Ben. I met him on match.com before match.com was even popular. He had a funny profile picture of himself holding up a glass of milk, although it was a bit blurred and far away I thought it was cute. I sent him a quick message and titled it Got Milk?. I told him I liked his picture and was hoping to get off of match.com soon and wondered if he could help me out.

My profile was cute. I had a picture of myself lying on a lounge chair at the pool. I wore a fun blue tank top and a huge smile. My hair, which was still a bit on the unmanageable side, was wet in the picture and looked terrific. I was in great shape and actually had a bikini hidden under that tank top.

Ben replied that same day and we scheduled our first date for the very next night. Ben was about 5'10" with a rock-hard body. He was not exactly my type, but it would work for now. His face was OK, kind of big with some old acne scars, but still cute. His tea-brown hair was cut short and lacked any kind of style. His clothes were generic and lacked style too. It didn't bother me enough to turn me off, just something I was conscious of. I thought it would be easily fixable with one quick trip to TJ Maxx.

We sat at a trendy bar in West Hartford Center and he was quite uncomfortable with his surroundings. We made small talk for about an hour. The conversation wasn't particularly exciting; in fact I grew tired of talking after about 30 minutes. But I thought he was very sexy, and I hadn't been with anyone since my divorce and was feeling ready to have a physical connection with this guy. I leaned over early in the date and touched his arm. It looked so huge I couldn't hold myself back. Even without flexing his muscles he looked bigger than any other man I ever dated. Almost like one of those cheesy Chippendale models from back in the 1980's.

We finished our drinks and he asked if I would like another drink. I declined and he requested the check. After the bill was paid Ben said he would really like to just come back to my condo and hang out with me. He said it was not about anything sexual but he just wanted a quiet place to chat and get to know me better. Note: this is a bad idea – don't try it! But I was brand-new to dating and dying to get this guy back to my condo. Ben followed me to my place, which was about two miles up the road. We entered my home and began making out before we even closed the front door. He pushed me down on the couch and we pressed our bodies together while we kissed for a good half hour.

As much as I was tempted to rip his clothes off and have sex on the middle of my living floor, I stopped the passion in the heat of the moment. I told Ben that I was sorry to lead him on but had no clue what I was doing and needed to cool things off. Ben was a true gentleman about the whole scene. We opened a bottle of wine and sat and talked on the couch for a couple of hours. The drunker we got the better the conversation got.

We kissed a few more times and realized it was 2:00 a.m. Ben was drunk and didn't want to drive home. He asked to sleep on the couch but I really wanted him in my bed. I put on some cute pajamas, nothing too sexy as I think I teased him enough for one date. I fell asleep spooned in his hard, muscular body. We woke up around 11 the next morning and went to breakfast, came home and took cozy nap together in my bed.

When we woke up, I made some sandwiches for lunch and the small talk started up again. By this time it was three in the afternoon and I only had two hours left before my son was due home from his father's house. I brought Ben up to my bedroom and had the best sex I had had in years. After, he was kind of funny and made some jokes about the marathon foreplay. Ben kissed me goodbye and said he would call.

Ben did call that following Tuesday night. We dated for eight weeks on a steady, consistent schedule. Matt was with his father every Wednesday and Saturday night and these turned into our regular date nights. We didn't exactly go on dates though. Ben would come to my house with a bottle of wine. We would rip each other's clothes off and have great sex for hours. We would lie in bed naked together until morning came around when he would say goodbye. He would only call the night before our encounters to confirm. There were never phone calls just to say hello, never emails and never an adjustment to the schedule. We rarely went out and never really talked about much of anything too personal.

Isn't it true that physical chemistry is important?

Yes, physical chemistry is very important and ours was intense. We definitely had a connection in the bedroom. But this chemistry is just not enough. Ben was emotionally unavailable. We talked about basic things. He asked me questions and I asked him questions but it always felt forced. I kept convincing myself that it was just new and he would open up soon enough. He was nice to me, reliable, consistent and good in bed. Surely this was enough to have a long-lasting relationship? NOT! Eight weeks of this became really annoying and I knew down deep that it would never change. I was bored and yearning to get back on match.com.

He arrived on his routine Saturday night date and I couldn't get through another night with him. I nicely ended the relationship and he drove off without a fight. Within the hour I logged back into my match.com profile and who was the first match that I saw? Ben! He was just as eager to get back on that site as I was. We were both trapped by the sex but when nothing else is there, the sex is only good for about eight weeks.

So what are the other things that you would need besides chemistry?

Well the two most important things are chemistry and respect but you can't stop there. Having someone that is physically and emotionally available is imperative. Sure, he was physically available two nights a week, but I wanted more. Make excuses all you want ladies. I did it with this guy and many others. I remember rationalizing that he lived far away, yet it was under an hour. I would remind myself that he worked hard during the week and always hits the gym after work so he just doesn't get a chance to call. Or he knows I have my son and must just figure I am busy with him. All excuses!

Ben did not care how my day was, what was new in my life or about my son. Nor did he have any interest in connecting with me in any way during the time that we were not physically together. Each week I thought maybe we would develop a closer connection. But each week came and each week went with the exact same pattern. Perhaps I could have initiated the question about where the relationship was headed or would we ever be able to see each other more frequently. I do remember calling him on a Monday night just because I was feeling lonely and wanted to connect. The only thing that call really did was confirm our Wednesday night hook-up two days early.

I tried and hoped somehow we would miraculously fall in love, but I got so bored. Sure, good sex was helpful in moving on from my divorce, but I knew I needed so much more. That is when I proudly sent Ben on his merry way.

Could it be true that their life circumstances or schedule just makes them less available?

The minute you start making excuses for a guy who is physically and/or emotionally unavailable, you need to remind yourself that it doesn't matter what the excuses are. You deserve to be with someone who wants to spend time with you and wants to connect with you even when you can't physically be together. With today's technology it takes seconds to send a quick text. And those few seconds send an enormous message to the person you are dating. Sure, there might be an occasion when you are dating a single dad who has his kids half of the time. And he may have to work quite hard as he is now paying child support and alimony. But if this guy was really into you, he would find the time to let you know you that he is thinking about you and that you are special. He would want to make it as easy as possible for you to stay interested during his physical absence so you wouldn't be tempted to stray and find someone else.

As far as the emotionally unavailable guy, they are a complete waste of time. You know, that guy who wants to take things slowly because he was hurt in the past. Perhaps his wife cheated on him, or he just got out of a painful relationship. Most of the time, guys are not that deep and it is just a lame excuse to say, "I want to have sex with you but please don't aggravate me about moving forward with this relationship." If a guy wants you bad enough he can get over the emotional scars from his break up quite quickly. And on the off-chance that I am wrong on this subject, do you really want to nurse a wounded man back health? It just sounds really unsexy to have a man crying and whining about his ex-wife. I thought we all wanted that guy with a little bit of an edge anyway – right?

Was there anything positive to come out of this relationship?

I actually had one other lesson from my crush with Ben. It is all related to the steamy sexual relationship that we had. Women so often suppress their sexual desires and fantasies. We feel like sluts if we have sex too early with someone. Women also waste time feeling self-conscious about their bodies, to the point where they don't even know what would pleasure them. I don't ever recommend having sex on the first date even if the date is 24 hours long. But I will say that if you are a woman and you are looking to just fulfill your sexual desires with a man than you deserve that under certain conditions.

First, safe sex is hugely important and I can't for the life of me imagine how any self-respecting woman can allow a man's penis inside of her without a condom on. Second, be sure that you can accept that the relationship is just sex. I truly knew down deep that Ben was not for me.

I remember after a few weeks of dating he asked me if I was using him for sex. I just laughed it off and a made a joke out of it, but to some extent it was true. I wasn't feeling those exciting feelings you have when you are falling for someone new. Having sex with him was all I really wanted, and I was OK with that. We had an agreement that we weren't having sex with anyone else, he wore a condom every time and I was enjoying every minute of sex with this man.

Also I was honest with him and ended the relationship before I went out and had sex with anyone else. Women, don't be ashamed of having sexual desires, don't suppress your fantasies and please enjoy your sexuality. If you hate sex, always say your sex drive is just very low or never have had an orgasm, you need to address this and figure out what it is that truly pleasures you.

So, in a nutshell, what do I need to do?

A physical connection with someone is just not enough to sustain a relationship. At the end of the day we all get old and our physical shell deteriorates. It changes shape, loses hair and wrinkles, among many other things, and the connection fades away. That is why it is so important to make an effort to see what is inside.

If the guy isn't emotionally guarded, he will allow you to see his soul, his emotional side. This is the part that doesn't have to deteriorate like the shell. In fact, the soul can improve over the years, and we actually have a tremendous amount of control over what happens to our souls! When you fall in love with the emotional part of a person, the love is so much stronger. I have seen many super-attractive couples date for about three months. Everyone talks about what a gorgeous couple they are and how beautiful their kids would be. Then, to everyone's shock, they break up. In most cases they never fell in love with each other's souls.

So before you claim to be in love with someone you are physically attracted to, be sure you understand their thoughts, appreciate their passions and love them for the true person that they are.

16 - ERIK

Every morning I would wake up, turn on my computer and log onto match.com. I did my routine search for new profiles. On this particular hot July morning, the first profile to pop up was titled "Blazman". He had a picture of himself wearing a Buffalo Sabres hockey shirt and appeared to be holding a mug of beer. Blazman was gorgeous with a sexy smile that just melted me. He was blonde 5'11" and lived in West Hartford, which was very appealing after dating Ben. I sent Blazman an email and wrote some comment about us being neighbors and suggested we plan to run into each other in West Hartford Center. He responded quickly to tell me he was out of town and would get back to me in a few days.

Blazman did get back to me with a quick email asking me when we were going to meet. I told him that Internet dating etiquette usually deemed a phone call before a live encounter. It was apparent that he was new to the whole online dating thing. So Blazman called me the next day and repeated his question about when we would meet. I quickly realized he was pretty direct, which was fine with me. I was getting sick of the 12 pen pals I had acquired on match.com who couldn't seem to commit to a date. We chatted briefly, I learned his name was Erik, he owned Sherpa Technologies (a web development company) and he had no trouble meeting women – he just had trouble meeting smart women, as he put it.

Erik was my thirteenth match.com date. We met at Baskin Robbins in West Hartford Center. Actually that is where I met the majority of my match.com dates. It was always a Wednesday night as that was the one night during the week that I didn't have my son with me. I showed up to Baskin Robbins almost every Wednesday night wearing the same outfit. The only difference was that the guy I met changed from week to week. I imagine the staff at Baskin Robbins were quite confused.

Erik came walking towards me and I felt the sparks flying. Those of you that have had Internet or blind dates know what happens as the date approaches you. You are either thinking, *please let this be him* or *no don't let this be him*. Well Erik was one of those dates that I was hoping was him.

Erik had blonde short hair, blue eyes and a gorgeous face. He was the first Polish guy I ever had a crush on. His features were strong and tough-looking. He approached me with a confident, sincere smile on his face. I was totally and instantly attracted to this guy! Here was a nice guy with enough of an edge to interest me! He had a Pitbull, played hockey and liked motorcycles. But at the same time we could have deep conversations about any topic. Our milkshake date lasted three hours. I always suggest first dates should be milkshake/handshake dates so no one spends a lot of money and no one wastes a whole lot of time. But with Erik I had no desire to leave.

We sat on a cement step in the middle of the Center and talked about everything from families to work to hobbies. I couldn't get enough of talking to him. Finally, everything was closing up around us and it seemed to force the date to end too. Erik walked me to the car and we actually had a kiss in the middle of the parking lot. I got in my car, grabbed my cell phone and called my best friend, Pauline. I told her this was it, he was perfect for me and I got to relive the whole date with her.

What was so cool about Erik was that I never had to question when I would hear from this guy. He was always present in my life. I remember hanging curtains one night and he called. My machine picked up and he left a message saying he was going for a bike ride, would be in my neighborhood and wanted to stop in. This was awesome - a guy who found a way to fit me in his life on a regular basis. We laughed all the time and he told me that my best feature was that I always had a smile on my face. I was falling in love with this guy.

About six weeks into the relationship, I took him to Cape Cod to meet my college roommates and my sister and brother-in-law. We went to a party with my whole crowd and everyone thought he was terrific. After the party I took Erik to the beach where my parents used to live. This is one of my favorite places in the whole world, as it always makes me feel closest to my mom. We talked, kissed and enjoyed the beautiful view. Later that night we went back to my sister's house to sleep. Erik and I began talking about past relationships. He told me that in the past he would often pull away when he'd start to fall in love with a girl. I said "I hope you don't do that with me" and Erik replied, "I didn't."

After one year of dating Erik my heart was broken. He said he was pretty sure that I was "the one" but he just wasn't ready. He needed to go back out and experience dating. In other words, he was no longer into me! I told him that I just might not be here when he is, in fact, ready. Erik said it was a risk he had to take.

I was "crushed"! I tried to go back on match.com, and no one even compared to Erik. He was so real, so funny and so not that interested in me anymore! I forced myself to go on a couple of lame dates and stayed in touch with Erik. He would come to my house during that summer break-up and we would hang out for hours. I fought every desire to be with him intimately because I just couldn't bear to go from his girlfriend to being part of his rotation, assuming he had a rotation.

At first it was hard; I thought about him constantly. I would check my cell phone and my email nonstop. As time went on, I thought about him less and less. I worked hard to stop focusing on how much I missed him and started focusing on my life. Sure, it is easier to fall into a trap of being miserable and depressed, but I was DONE being a victim. I needed a vacation and Matthew and I packed our bags and took off to see my dad in Florida. It was great to be away and I had longer and longer bouts of not thinking about Erik. I logged onto match.com from my dad's house in Florida and even lined up a date to make coming home more inviting.

It was about two hours after I arrived home from a great visit with my dad that Erik called me. He invited me over and reluctantly I went. We lied on the couch for hours together and didn't talk a whole lot. But we were somehow connected like no time had passed. We missed each other and weren't afraid to show it. I don't remember Erik ever putting it into words but it was clear that he wanted me back in his life and not just for that night. Erik and I started dating again and were together constantly. I was happy! I loved myself and I loved Erik.

A year and half later, Erik and I took off to Las Vegas and were married with his two best friends as our witnesses. He and his Pitbull Shelly moved into my beautiful home in West Hartford, CT. Matthew adjusted to the new additions to our family and really did begin to love his step dad.

After a few years, I told my husband that he needed to have a child of his own. Erik is almost five years younger than me and I didn't want him to decide later on that he wanted a child. I was in my late 30's and my clock was ticking fast.

We decided to give it one shot and if it was meant to be than it was meant to be. Nine months later our beautiful baby boy, Trevor Huck, was born and our lives haven't been the same since. I look out the window at the boys shooting basketball, chopping wood and wrestling and I have to pinch myself to be sure it is all real. And it is all real. It was a tremendous journey to get to a place of such joy and I am so happy for every experience along the way because this is where I landed.

I am completely and fully in love with myself, my husband, my children and my life. I know making everyone sick is not exactly the best way to end my book. But I am so tired of hearing about people in miserable unfulfilling marriages. These people actually make it their mission to preach to others that all marriages are miserable and it is not true!

Does true love really exist? Can you really find someone terrific and not have to sacrifice anything?

True love is real and you should never settle for anything less. I admit there are days that Erik annoys me and we have some good arguments from time to time. I wish the dishes would be washed more often and I am always finding his dirty socks under the bed and buried in the sheets. And it can be a bit annoying when he comes to bed at 2:00 AM and wakes me. But this is the truth. After ten years of dating, seven years of marriage and raising two children together, I love this man with my heart and soul.

When I pull into the driveway at the end of a long day I smile if his car is in the driveway. When our cars pass on the road I still get butterflies in my stomach. And when he winks at me across the room I blush. When Erik climbs into bed at night, no matter how tired I am, I still feel joy knowing that he is next to me. Whenever anything of importance happens in my life he is the first person I share it with.

Sometimes Erik claims I talk too much. But we have an arrangement. He loves to have his back and shoulders rubbed and I love to talk. So when I have a big story that I want to share that may be a bit boring for Erik to sit through, he gestures me to me to rub his back. We both chuckle and I rub until I have finished my stories. In fact I sat rubbing his back for hours while I read "Crush" to him from start to finish. He would interrupt me from time to time to share a grammatical error, or to tell me to move a little lower or to the left shoulder as opposed to the right one.

There is no home in the world filled with more love than ours. The four of us sit at that dinner table and play a game we invented called "minutia" where we all share something in our day that qualifies as menial or uneventful. We put the music on and dance, despite my complete lack of rhythm. Cookies are often baking in the oven, neighborhood kids are always at the door and you just never know what you will find us doing on a random night of the week. We are not the family that sits in front of the TV for endless hours. We are home together, happy and always present in each other's lives.

Does he have a brother?

Nope, sorry ladies he does not have a brother. But I can assure you that you too can find such happiness.

In a nutshell what is the most important thing we need to know?

To all those people that convince themselves that marriage is hard, that most people stop having sex after a few years and that you have to work at it all the time, they are wrong. Marriage is wonderful, happy couples do still exist and it is not constant work. Of course you need to communicate and respect each other. And there are many ups and down in any relationship. But when you are both happy and both love yourselves first you can have a happy ending!

CONCLUSION

When I finished writing this book my 11 year old son Matthew asked me if there was going to be a "Crush 2". I laughed and said that I hope not! Although I don't have a single regret I would be quite content with Erik being my last and final crush.

We all make mistakes and as you can see I have made many. But when a mistake is made you have a choice. You can learn from it, deny it or waste energy feeling guilty about it. If you are single and hoping to find true love I challenge you to relive some of your biggest crushes. Even relive the ones that feel badly. I relived Vinnie so you can do this too. But don't think about what a jerk the guy was or what a fool you were to fall for him. Just think about what lessons you can learn from each and every one of those crushes. Because there are so many lessons to be learned from your lifetime of crushes.

I hope my thoughts will help you to recognize that you deserve nothing less than true happiness. And at the end of the day the two words I hope you carry with you forever are "never settle."

ABOUT THE AUTHOR

Jaimy, also known as The Date Doctor, has been helping folks find true love since she started her own dating company in 2005. Her speed dating and singles events have been very successful in helping those who are ready for love, find just that. Today you can catch her candid and direct advice on the Damon Scott Show on 96.5 TIC FM. She also has a weekly segment on Better CT. Jaimy and her husband produce and host a Sunday night podcast called, The Date Doctor Podcast where they answer your questions about love, dating and relationships.

Jaimy lives with her husband, Erik and two sons, Matthew and Trevor in West Hartford, CT.

27640844R00067

Made in the USA
Charleston, SC
17 March 2014